THE
PRINCE'S
CHOICE

THE PRINCE'S CHOICE

*A Personal Selection from
Shakespeare with an Introduction by*
THE PRINCE OF WALES

Hodder & Stoughton

Copyright in this selection and introduction © A. G. Carrick Ltd 1995
Copyright in introduction to individual extracts © Hodder and Stoughton
Copyright in the extracts from Shakespeare © Oxford University Press 1988
Copyright in the lyrics to 'Brush Up Your Shakespeare' © 1968 Porter, Cole, Buxton-Hill-Music Corp, USA, Warner Chappell Music Ltd, London W1Y 3FA. Reproduced by permission of IMP Ltd.

First published in 1995 by Hodder and Stoughton
A division of Hodder Headline PLC

All quotations from Shakespeare are taken from
THE OXFORD SHAKESPEARE The Complete Works, edited by Stanley Wells and Gary Taylor, published by Oxford University Press, with their kind permission.

The right of His Royal Highness The Prince of Wales to be identified as the Author of the Introduction to this work has been asserted in accordance with the Copyright Designs and Patents Act 1988

10 9 8 7 6 5 4 3 2 1

A CIP catalogue record for this title is available from the British Library.

ISBN 0 340 66039 2

Photoset by Rowland Phototypesetting Ltd,
Bury St Edmunds, Suffolk
Printed and bound in Great Britain by
Mackays of Chatham PLC, Chatham, Kent
Designed by Behram Kapadia

Hodder and Stoughton Ltd
A division of Hodder Headline PLC
338 Euston Road
London NW1 3BH

CONTENTS

CONTENTS

INTRODUCTION

My acquaintance with Shakespeare began in singularly undistinguished fashion. The O-level text we ground our way through at Gordonstoun was *Julius Caesar*. The experience left me largely unmoved. It was only quite recently that I re-read the play and appreciated for the first time the fascination of that complex character Brutus, the reluctant revolutionary; the excitement and rhetoric of Antony's great speeches, and the extraordinary timelessness of Shakespeare's presentation and analysis of riot, revolution, intrigue and internecine strife which is at the heart of the play.

One of the problems, I suspect, was that at first I failed to realise just what fun Shakespeare could be.

> Brush up your Shakespeare
> Start quoting him now.
> Brush up your Shakespeare
> And the women you will wow.
>
> Just declaim a few lines from Othella
> And they'll think you're a helluva fella.
> If your blonde won't respond when you flatter 'er
> Tell her what Tony told Cleopater-er.

> And if still to be shocked she pretends, well
> Just remind her that 'All's well that ends well'.

Such was the advice given by Cole Porter, that twentieth-century master of popular culture, in his musical, *Kiss Me Kate*. Cole Porter's teasingly affectionate acknowledgement that you can have fun with Shakespeare seems to me to be something which each generation has to discover anew for itself.

All of us who have been fortunate enough to develop an acquaintance with, and love of, Shakespeare have our favourite plays. One of mine happens to be *Henry V*. This probably has something to do with the fact that it was the first Shakespearian play in which I was able to play a part. As the Duke of Exeter, I was allowed one rather splendid speech at the French court, but then faded from view, apart from a couple of reappearances on the battlefield at Agincourt and a modest walk-on role in the final scene.

I have seen the play a few times since then. I was spellbound by Kenneth Branagh's performance at Stratford and I have seen his film of *Henry V* at least three times. Some find it a rather jingoistic play, glorifying war. Certainly there are great speeches of resolute action. But each time I have seen or read the play, it has been the humanity of the King that has moved me most.

> Upon the King.
> 'Let us our lives, our souls, our debts, our care-full wives,
> Our children, and our sins, lay on the King.'
> We must bear all. O hard condition,
> Twin-born with greatness: subject to the breath
> Of every fool, whose sense no more can feel
> But his own wringing. What infinite heartsease
> Must kings neglect that private men enjoy?
> And what have kings that privates have not too,
> Save ceremony, save general ceremony?

When I re-read this play nearly twenty years after performing in it at school, I found myself wondering in amazement at

Shakespeare's insight into the mind of someone born into this kind of position.

Of course, that speech from *Henry V* is not just about the innermost concerns of kings. It is about the loneliness of high office, the responsibilities and stresses which afflict all those who shoulder great burdens, run industries or schools – or perhaps nurse invalided relatives.

One of the unique qualities of Shakespeare – which has, like every other aspect of his genius, survived for four hundred years – is his all-encompassing view of mankind. All human life really is there, with an extraordinary range and subtlety of characterisation, of historical setting, of place. His understanding of domestic life, of the minds of soldiers and politicians, of the fundamental relationships between men and women was so vast that it remains eternally relevant. Consider this recent statement from Francis Bacon, proclaimed by the media as the greatest English painter since Turner:

> I think that man now realises that he is an accident, that he is a completely futile being, that he has to play out the game without reason. . . . You see, all art has now become completely a game by which man distracts himself; and you may say that it has always been like that, but now it is entirely a game.

Now contrast it with this passage from *Hamlet*:

> What a piece of work is a man! How noble in reason, how infinite in faculty, in form and moving how express and admirable, in action how like an angel, in apprehension how like a god – the beauty of the world, the paragon of animals!

Which of those views of man is nearer the truth?

Time and again in Shakespeare's characters we recognise elements of ourselves. Shakespeare has that ability to draw characters so universal that we find them alive and around us today, every day of our lives. Shakespeare was a consummate technician and psychologist, with a remarkable ability to understand what makes us all what we are.

His plays are the direct successors of the Mystery plays, so popular in later medieval Europe, which deliberately set out to hand on to future generations essential knowledge and experience under the guise of entertainment. Like them, Shakespeare's plays communicate wisdom through the evocation and study of human emotion, thought and behaviour.

Shakespeare holds the mirror up to Nature for us to see ourselves and to experience ourselves, so that we gain in the process a more profound understanding of ourselves and others, appreciating right and wrong, and the laws of emotion and nature which make us behave as we do.

Art in its broadest sense provides us with access to some of the essential truths about the meaning and significance of life. Artists – and again I use the term in its widest possible sense – have a unique capacity to illustrate, to educate and to inspire. It is the poet who reveals to us true beauty in, for example, Enobarbus's glorious description of Cleopatra:

The barge she sat in, like a burnished throne
Burned on the water. The poop was beaten gold;
Purple the sails, and so perfumèd that
The winds were love-sick with them. The oars were silver,
Which to the tune of flutes kept stroke, and made
The water which they beat to follow faster,
As amorous of their strokes. For her own person,
It beggared all description.

In the same way, it is the painter who gives depth to those everyday items so familiar that we fail to appreciate them. It is the pen of the cartoonist or satirist which lays bare the hypocrisy and deceit with which people seek to camouflage their real intentions. Art is concerned with truth and morality as well as with beauty. Shelley had it right two hundred years ago: 'Poets are the unacknowledged legislators of the world.'

I am one of those who believe that man's mind is more than a mere mechanical object functioning in a mechanistic world which has evolved from the clockwork universe of Newton to the computer models now deemed to possess artificial intelligence. Despite all the dramatic changes that have been wrought by science and technology, and the remarkable benefits they have brought us, there remains deep in the soul of each of us, I believe, a vital metaphysical ingredient which makes life worth living. This awareness of a spiritual dimension greater than, and beyond, the confines of our everyday self, has a particular link to aesthetic experience, and great literature offers one of the keys to understanding that truth, and to understanding ourselves. There is a marvellous, definitive rejection of the rootless, soulless, mechanistic view of man in *The Merchant of Venice*:

> The man that hath no music in himself,
> Nor is not moved with concord of sweet sounds,
> Is fit for treasons, stratagems and spoils.
> The motions of his spirit are dull as night,
> And his affections dark as Erebus:
> Let no such man be trusted.

For those of us who speak English it is our enormous good fortune that the world's greatest playwright – perhaps the world's greatest poet – wrote in our own language. Whether we realise it or not, Shakespeare is a part of our daily lives. We all shake our heads in despair, 'more in sorrow than in anger', and gardeners like me throughout the country wonder why even the fullest respect for organic principles produces 'things rank and gross in nature' in our flower beds.

Shakespeare's language is ours, his roots are ours, his culture is ours – brought up as he was in the gentle Warwickshire countryside, educated at the grammar school in Stratford, baptized and buried in the local church. His message, however, is a universal, timeless one. He is not just our poet, but the world's.

I can lay no claim to scholarly expertise, but I love Shakespeare. My time as president of the Renaissance Theatre Company and of the Royal Shakespeare Company, most of whose productions I try to see each season, has given me real pleasure. I hope this little anthology may remind its readers of the delights of Shakespeare and inspire some of them to re-read the plays or, better still, to see them again on the stage.

PROLOGUE

AS YOU LIKE IT

Act II: Scene 7.

*Duke Senior and his lords, including Jaques the court philosopher,
prepare to dine on their frugal meal in the forest when the runaway
Orlando invades their al fresco refectory with his sword drawn. His
miserable state and the privations which he and his faithful old
servant Adam have had to endure cause the Duke to moralise upon
the unhappy lot of mankind. Seizing his cue, Jaques advances the
argument and divides human existence, from birth to death, into
the Seven Ages of Man.*

Jaques: All the world's a stage,
      And all the men and women merely players.
      They have their exits and their entrances,
      And one man in his time plays many parts,
      His acts being seven ages. At first the infant,
      Mewling and puking in the nurse's arms.
      Then the whining schoolboy with his satchel
      And shining morning face, creeping like snail
      Unwillingly to school. And then the lover,
      Sighing like a furnace, with a woeful ballad
      Made to his mistress' eyebrow. Then, a soldier,
      Full of strange oaths, and bearded like the pard,
      Jealous in honour, sudden, and quick in
          quarrel,
      Seeking the bubble reputation
      Even in the cannon's mouth. And then the
          justice,
      In fair round belly with good capon lined,
      With eyes severe and beard of formal cut,
      Full of wise saws and modern instances;
      And so he plays his part. The sixth age shifts
      Into the lean and slippered pantaloon,
      With spectacles on nose and pouch on side,
      His youthful hose, well saved, a world too
          wide

For his shrunk shank, and his big, manly voice,
Turning again toward childish treble, pipes
And whistles in his sound. Last scene of all,
That ends this strange, eventful history,
Is second childishness and mere oblivion,
Sans teeth, sans eyes, sans taste, sans
   everything.

EXTRAORDINARY
PEOPLE
AND
EXCEPTIONAL
LANGUAGE

'We seem to have forgotten that for solemn occasions we need exceptional and solemn language: something which transcends our everyday speech. We commend the "beauty of holiness"; yet we forget the holiness of beauty. If we encourage the use of mean, trite, ordinary language we encourage a mean, trite and ordinary view of the world we inhabit.'

Prince Charles, Thomas Cranmer Schools Prize Speech, 1989.

ANTONY AND CLEOPATRA

ACT II: SCENE 2.

Leaving Cleopatra in Egypt, Antony has returned to Rome to be reconciled with Octavius Caesar. Lepidus, the third member of the triumvirate which rules the Roman world, suggests that the alliance would be strengthened if Antony were to marry Caesar's sister, Octavia. While negotiations proceed offstage, Agrippa and Maecenas, two of Caesar's intimates, eagerly press questions on Enobarbus, Antony's right-hand man, about the fabled Cleopatra. Enobarbus vividly describes the brilliance and the drama of the first, fateful meeting of Antony and Cleopatra.

Enobarbus: The barge she sat in, like a burnished throne
      Burned on the water. The poop was beaten
        gold;
      Purple the sails, and so perfumed that
      The winds were love-sick with them. The oars
        were silver,
      Which to the tune of flutes kept stroke, and
        made
      The water which they beat to follow faster,
      As amorous of their strokes. For her own
        person,
      It beggared all description. She did lie
      In her pavilion – cloth of gold, of tissue –
      O'er-picturing that Venus where we see
      The fancy outwork nature. On each side her
      Stood pretty dimpled boys, like smiling
        Cupids,
      With divers-coloured fans whose wind did
        seem
      To glow the delicate cheeks which they did
        cool,
      And what they undid did.

Agrippa: O, rare for Antony!
Enobarbus: Her gentlewomen, like the Nereides,

13

So many mermaids, tended her i'th' eyes,
And made their bends adornings. At the helm
A seeming mermaid steers. The silken tackle
Swell with the touches of those flower-soft
   hands
That yarely frame the office. From the barge
A strange invisible perfume hits the sense
Of the adjacent wharfs. The city cast
Her people out upon her, and Antony,
Enthroned i'th' market-place, did sit alone,
Whistling to th' air, which but for vacancy
Had gone to gaze on Cleopatra too,
And made a gap in nature.

Agrippa: Rare Egyptian!
Enorbarbus: Upon her landing Antony sent to her,
Invited her to supper. She replied
It should be better he became her guest,
Which she entreated. Our courteous Antony,
Whom ne'er the word of 'No' woman heard
   speak,
Being barbered ten times o'er, goes to the feast,
And for his ordinary pays his heart
For what his eyes eat only.

Agrippa: Royal wench!
She made great Caesar lay his sword to bed.
He ploughed her, and she cropped.

Enobarbus: I saw her once
Hop forty paces through the public street,
And having lost her breath, she spoke and
   panted,
That she did make defect perfection,
And breathless, pour breath forth.

Maecenas: Now Antony
Must leave her utterly.

Enobarbus: Never. He will not.
Age cannot wither her, nor custom stale
Her infinite variety. Other women cloy
The appetites they feed, but she makes hungry

Where most she satisfies. For vilest things
Become themselves in her, that the holy priests
Bless her when she is riggish.

ANTONY AND CLEOPATRA

Act II: Scene 5.

*While Antony makes a political marriage in Rome with Octavia,
Cleopatra waits impatiently in Alexandria for news of his
impending return. Her fond reminiscences of her life with Antony
are interrupted by the arrival of a messenger from Rome. The
volatile Queen's mood changes: she rains questions on the terrified
messenger and then assaults him when she learns that her lover has
married Octavia.*

Cleopatra:	Give me mine angle. We'll to th' river. There,
	My music playing far off, I will betray
	Tawny-finned fishes. My bended hook shall
	pierce
	Their slimy jaws, and as I draw them up
	I'll think them every one an Antony,
	And say 'Ah ha, you're caught!'
Charmian:	'Twas merry when
	You wagered on your angling, when your diver
	Did hang a salt fish on his hook, which he
	With fervency drew up.
Cleopatra:	That time – O times! –
	I laughed him out of patience, and that night
	I laughed him into patience, and next morn,
	Ere the ninth hour, I drunk him to his bed,
	Then put my tires and mantles on him whilst
	I wore his sword Philippan.
	Enter a Messenger
Cleopatra:	O, from Italy.
	Ram thou thy fruitful tidings in mine ears,
	That long time have been barren.
Messenger:	Madam, madam!
Cleopatra:	Antonio's dead. If thou say so, villain,
	Thou kill'st thy mistress; but well and free,
	If thou so yield him, there is gold, and here
	My bluest veins to kiss – a hand that kings

	Have lipped, and trembled kissing.
Messenger:	First, madam, he is well.
Cleopatra:	Why, there's more gold. But, sirrah, mark: we use
	To say the dead are well. Bring it to that,
	The gold I give thee will I melt and pour
	Down thy ill-uttering throat.
Messenger:	Good madam, hear me.
Cleopatra:	Well, go to, I will.
	But there's no goodness in thy face. If Antony
	Be free and healthful, so tart a favour
	To trumpet such good tidings! If not well,
	Thou shouldst come like a Fury crowned with snakes,
	Not like a formal man.
Messenger:	Will't please you hear me?
Cleopatra:	I have a mind to strike thee ere thou speak'st.
	Yet if thou say Antony lives, is well,
	Or friends with Caesar, or not captive to him,
	I'll set thee in a shower of gold, and hail
	Rich pearls upon thee.
Messenger:	Madam, he's well.
Cleopatra:	Well said.
Messenger:	And friends with Caesar.
Cleopatra:	Thou'rt an honest man.
Messenger:	Caesar and he are greater friends than ever.
Cleopatra:	Make thee a fortune from me.
Messenger:	But yet, madam –
Cleopatra:	I do not like 'But yet'; it does allay
	The good precedence. Fie upon 'But yet'.
	'But yet' is as a jailer to bring forth
	Some monstrous malefactor. Prithee, friend,
	Pour out the pack of matter to mine ear,
	The good and bad together. He's friends with Caesar,
	In state of health, thou sayst; and, thou sayst, free.

Messenger:	Free, madam? No, I made no such report.
	He's bound unto Octavia.
Cleopatra:	For what good turn?
Messenger:	For the best turn i'th' bed.
Cleopatra:	I am pale, Charmian.
Messenger:	Madam, he's married to Octavia.
Cleopatra:	The most infectious pestilence upon thee!
	She strikes him down
Messenger:	Good madam, patience!
Cleopatra:	What say you?
	She strikes him
	Hence, horrible villain, or I'll spurn thine eyes
	Like balls before me. I'll unhair thy head,
	She hales him up and down
	Thou shalt be whipped with wire and stewed in brine,
	Smarting in ling'ring pickle.
Messenger:	Gracious madam,
	I that do bring the news made not the match.
Cleopatra:	Say 'tis not so, a province I will give thee,
	And make thy fortunes proud. The blow thou hadst
	Shall make thy peace for moving me to rage,
	And I will boot thee with what gift beside
	Thy modesty can beg.
Messenger:	He's married, madam.
Cleopatra:	Rogue, thou hast lived too long.
	She draws a knife
Messenger:	Nay then, I'll run.
	What mean you, madam? I have made no fault.
	Exit
Charmian:	Good madam, keep yourself within yourself.
	The man is innocent.
Cleopatra:	Some innocents 'scape not the thunderbolt.
	Melt Egypt into Nile, and kindly creatures
	Turn all to serpents! Call the slave again.
	Though I am mad I will not bite him. Call!
Charmian:	He is afeard to come.

Cleopatra:	I will not hurt him.

Exit Charmian

These hands do lack nobility that they strike
A meaner than myself, since I myself
Have given myself the cause.

Enter the Messenger again with Charmian

Come hither, sir.
Though it be honest, it is never good
To bring bad news. Give to a gracious message
An host of tongues, but let ill tidings tell
Themselves when they be felt.

Messenger: I have done my duty.
Cleopatra: Is he married?
I cannot hate thee worser than I do
If thou again say 'Yes'.

Messenger: He's married, madam.
Cleopatra: The gods confound thee! Dost thou hold there
still?

Messenger: Should I lie, madam?
Cleopatra: O, I would thou didst,
So half my Egypt were submerged and made
A cistern for scaled snakes. Go, get thee hence.
Hadst thou Narcissus in thy face, to me
Thou wouldst appear most ugly. He is married?

Messenger: I crave your highness' pardon.
Cleopatra: He is married?
Messenger: Take no offence that I would not offend you.
To punish me for what you make me do
Seems much unequal. He's married to Octavia.

Cleopatra: O that his fault should make a knave of thee,
That act not what thou'rt sure of! Get thee hence.
The merchandise which thou hast brought from
Rome
Are all too dear for me. Lie they upon thy
hand,
And be undone by 'em.

Exit Messenger

Charmian: Good your highness, patience.

Cleopatra:	In praising Antony I have dispraised Caesar.
Charmian:	Many times, madam.
Cleopatra:	I am paid for't now. Lead me from hence.

I faint. O Iras, Charmian – 'tis no matter.
Go to the fellow, good Alexas, bid him
Report the feature of Octavia: her years,
Her inclination; let him not leave out
The colour of her hair. Bring me word quickly.

Exit Alexas

Let him for ever go – let him not, Charmian;
Though he be painted one way like a Gorgon,
The other way's a Mars. *(To Mardian)* Bid you
    Alexas
Bring me word how tall she is. Pity me,
    Charmian,
But do not speak to me. Lead me to my
    chamber.

CORIOLANUS

Act V: Scene 4.

*The army of Rome's mortal enemies the Volscians is encamped
outside the city, ready to strike at any moment. Its general is
Coriolanus, once Rome's greatest soldier but banished for his
overweening arrogance by a cabal headed by the Tribunes of the
People, Junius Brutus and Sicinius Velutus. Now, faced by the
consequences of his policy, a seriously alarmed Sicinius seeks
the help of Menenius, once the mentor of the youthful Coriolanus.
But the elder statesman can offer no comfort – the vengeance of
Martius Coriolanus is implacable.*

Menenius:	See you yon coign o'th' Capitol, yon cornerstone?
Sicinius:	Why, what of that?
Menenius:	If it be possible for you to displace it with your little finger, there is some hope the ladies of Rome, especially his mother, may prevail with him. But I say there is no hope in't, our throats are sentenced and stay upon execution.
Sicinius:	Is't possible that so short a time can alter the condition of a man?
Menenius:	There is difference between a grub and a butterfly, yet your butterfly was a grub. This Martius is grown from man to dragon. He has wings, he's more than a creeping thing.
Sicinius:	He loved his mother dearly.
Menenius:	So did he me, and he no more remembers his mother now than an eight-year-old horse. The tartness of his face sours ripe grapes. When he walks, he moves like an engine, and the ground shrinks before his treading. He is able to pierce a corslet with his eye, talks like a knell, and his 'hmh!' is a battery. He sits in his state as a thing made for Alexander. What he bids be done is finished with his bidding. He

23

	wants nothing of a god but eternity and a heaven to throne in.
Sicinius:	Yes: mercy, if you report him truly.
Menenius:	I paint him in the character. Mark what mercy his mother shall bring from him. There is no more mercy in him than there is milk in a male tiger. That shall our poor city find; and all this is 'long of you.
Sicinius:	The gods be good unto us!
Menenius:	No, in such a case the gods will not be good unto us. When we banished him we respected not them, and, he returning to break our necks, they respect not us.

CORIOLANUS

Act V: Scene 3.

Coriolanus holds court in his tent with Aufidius, once his bitterest foe but now his ally in the siege of his native city, boasting how impervious he has proved to the entreaties of the Romans. But the sight of his wife, young son and especially of his indomitable mother Volumnia all on their knees in supplication before him melts his resolution. The bitter reproaches of the mother who so profoundly shaped him causes a change of heart, even though Coriolanus is well aware that the lifting of the siege will shortly prove fatal to him.

Coriolanus:	My wife comes foremost, then the honoured mould
	Wherein this trunk was framed, and in her hand
	The grandchild to her blood. But out, affection!
	All bond and privilege of nature break;
	Let it be virtuous to be obstinate.
	Virgilia curtsies
	What is that curtsy worth? Or those dove's eyes
	Which can make gods forsworn? I melt, and am not
	Of stronger earth than others.
	Volumnia bows
	My mother bows,
	As if Olympus to a molehill should
	In supplication nod; and my young boy
	Hath an aspect of intercession which
	Great nature cries 'Deny not'. – Let the Volsces
	Plough Rome and harrow Italy! I'll never
	Be such a gosling to obey instinct, but stand
	As if a man were author of himself
	And knew no other kin.
Virgilia:	My lord and husband.
Coriolanus:	These eyes are not the same I wore in Rome.

Virgilia:	The sorrow that delivers us thus changed
	Makes you think so.
Coriolanus:	Like a dull actor now
	I have forgot my part, and I am out
	Even to a full disgrace. *(Rising)* Best of my
	flesh,
	Forgive my tyranny, but do not say
	For that 'Forgive our Romans'.
	Virgilia kisses him
	O, a kiss
	Long as my exile, sweet as my revenge!
	Now, by the jealous queen of heaven, that kiss
	I carried from thee, dear, and my true lip
	Hath virgined it e'er since. You gods, I prate,
	And the most noble mother of the world
	Leave unsaluted! Sink, my knee, i'th' earth.
	He kneels
	Of thy deep duty more impression show
	Than that of common sons.
Virgilia:	O, stand up blest,
	Coriolanus rises
	Whilst with no softer cushion than the flint
	I kneel before thee, and unproperly
	Show duty as mistaken all this while
	Between the child and parent.
	She kneels
Coriolanus:	What's this?
	Your knees to me? To your corrected son?
	He raises her
	Then let the pebbles on the hungry beach
	Fillip the stars; then let the mutinous winds
	Strike the proud cedars 'gainst the fiery sun,
	Murd'ring impossibility to make
	What cannot be slight work.
Volumnia:	Thou art my warrior.
	I holp to frame thee. Do you know this lady?
Coriolanus:	The noble sister of Publicola,
	The moon of Rome, chaste as the icicle

	That's candied by the frost from purest snow
	And hangs on Dian's temple – dear Valeria!
Volumnia:	*(showing Coriolanus his son)* This is a poor epitome of yours,
	Which by th' interpretation of full time
	May show like all yourself.
Coriolanus:	*(to Young Martius)* The god of soldiers,
	With the consent of supreme Jove, inform
	Thy thoughts with nobleness, that thou mayst prove
	To shame unvulnerable, and stick i'th' wars
	Like a great sea-mark standing every flaw
	And saving those that eye thee!
Volumnia:	*(to Young Martius)* Your knee, sirrah.
	Young Martius kneels
Coriolanus:	That's my brave boy.
Volumnia:	Even he, your wife, this lady, and myself
	Are suitors to you.
Coriolanus:	I beseech you, peace.
	Or if you'd ask, remember this before:
	The things I have forsworn to grant may never
	Be held by you denials. Do not bid me
	Dismiss my soldiers, or capitulate
	Again with Rome's mechanics. Tell me not
	Wherein I seem unnatural. Desire not t'allay
	My rages and revenges with your colder reasons.
Volumnia:	O, no more, no more!
	You have said you will not grant us anything –
	For we have nothing else to ask but that
	Which you deny already. Yet we will ask,
	That, if you fail in our request, the blame
	May hang upon your hardness. Therefore hear us.
Coriolanus:	Aufidius and you Volsces, mark, for we'll
	Hear naught from Rome in private.
	He sits
	Your request?

27

Volumnia: Should we be silent and not speak, our raiment
And state of bodies would bewray what life
We have led since thy exile. Think with thyself
How more unfortunate than all living women
Are we come hither, since that thy sight, which
should
Make our eyes flow with joy, hearts dance with
comforts,
Constrains them weep and shake with fear and
sorrow,
Making the mother, wife, and child to see
The son, the husband, and the father tearing
His country's bowels out; and to poor we
Thine enmity's most capital. Thou barr'st us
Our prayers to the gods, which is a comfort
That all but we enjoy. For how can we,
Alas, how can we for our country pray,
Whereto we are bound, together with thy
victory,
Whereto we are bound? Alack, or we must lose
The country, our dear nurse, or else thy
person,
Our comfort in the country. We must find
An evident calamity, though we had
Our wish which side should win. For either
thou
Must as a foreign recreant be led
With manacles thorough our streets, or else
Triumphantly tread on thy country's ruin,
And bear the palm for having bravely shed
Thy wife and children's blood. For myself, son,
I purpose not to wait on fortune till
These wars determine. If I cannot persuade
thee
Rather to show a noble grace to both parts
Than seek the end of one, thou shalt no sooner
March to assault thy country than to tread –
Trust to't, thou shalt not – on thy mother's womb

	That brought thee to this world.
Virgilia:	Ay, and mine,

That brought you forth this boy to keep your
    name
Living to time.

Young Martius: A shall not tread on me.
          I'll run away till I am bigger, but then I'll fight.

Coriolanus: Not of a woman's tenderness to be
          Requires nor child nor woman's face to see.
          I have sat too long.

          He rises and turns away

Volumnia: Nay, go not from us thus.
If it were so that our request did tend
To save the Romans, thereby to destroy
The Volsces whom you serve, you might
    condemn us
As poisonous of your honour. No, our suit
Is that you reconcile them: while the Volsces
May say 'This mercy we have showed', the
    Romans
'This we received', and each in either side
Give the all-hail to thee and cry 'Be blest
For making up this peace!' Thou know'st, great
    son,
The end of war's uncertain; but this certain
That if thou conquer Rome, the benefit
Which thou shalt thereby reap is such a name
Whose repetition will be dogged with curses,
Whose chronicle thus writ: 'The man was
    noble,
But with his last attempt he wiped it out,
Destroyed his country, and his name remains
To th' ensuing age abhorred.' Speak to me,
    son.
Thou hast affected the fine strains of honour,
To imitate the graces of the gods,
To tear with thunder the wide cheeks o'th' air,
And yet to charge thy sulphur with a bolt

That should but rive an oak. Why dost not
    speak?
Think'st thou it honourable for a noble man
Still to remember wrongs? Daughter, speak
    you,
He cares not for your weeping. Speak thou,
    boy.
Perhaps thy childishness will move him more
Than can our reasons. There's no man in the
    world
More bound to's mother, yet here he lets me
    prate
Like one i'th' stocks. Thou hast never in thy life
Showed thy dear mother any courtesy,
When she, poor hen, fond of no second brood
Has clucked thee to the wars and safely home,
Loaden with honour. Say my request's unjust,
And spurn me back. But if it be not so,
Thou art not honest, and the gods will plague
    thee
That thou restrain'st from me the duty which
To a mother's part belongs. – He turns away.
Down, ladies. Let us shame him with our
    knees.
To his surname 'Coriolanus' 'longs more pride
Than pity to our prayers. Down! An end.
This is the last.
       The ladies and Young Martius kneel
                So we will home to Rome,
And die among our neighbours. – Nay,
    behold's.
This boy, that cannot tell what he would have,
But kneels and holds up hands for fellowship,
Does reason our petition with more strength
Than thou hast to deny't. – Come, let us go.
This fellow had a Volscian to his mother.
His wife is in Corioles, and this child
Like him by chance. – Yet give us our dispatch.

I am hushed until our city be afire,
And then I'll speak a little.
He holds her by the hand, silent

Coriolanus: O mother, mother!
What have you done? Behold, the heavens do
    ope,
The gods look down, and this unnatural scene
They laugh at. O my mother, mother, O!
You have won a happy victory to Rome;
But for your son, believe it, O believe it,
Most dangerously you have with him
    prevailed,
If not most mortal to him. But let it come.
The ladies and Young Martius rise

MACBETH

ACT II: SCENE 1 AND SCENE 2.

It is past midnight. The feast in Macbeth's castle has broken up and King Duncan has retired to bed, full of praise for the welcome he has received. Macbeth, driven on by Lady Macbeth, has steeled himself to murder the King, but as he awaits her signal, his over-wrought mind conjures up the image of a dagger leading him towards Duncan's chamber.

Macbeth: Is this a dagger which I see before me,
The handle toward my hand? Come, let me
   clutch thee.
I have thee not, and yet I see thee still.
Art thou not, fatal vision, sensible
To feeling as to sight? Or art thou but
A dagger of the mind, a false creation,
Proceeding from the heat-oppressèd brain?
I see thee yet, in form as palpable
As this which now I draw.
Thou marshall'st me the way that I was going,
And such an instrument I was to use.
Mine eyes are made the fools o'th' other
   senses,
Or else worth all the rest. I see thee still,
And on thy blade and dudgeon gouts of blood,
Which was not so before. There's no such
   thing.
It is the bloody business which informs
Thus to mine eyes. Now o'er the one half-
   world
Nature seems dead, and wicked dreams abuse
The curtained sleep. Witchcraft celebrates
Pale Hecate's offerings and withered murder,
Alarumed by his sentinel the wolf,
Whose howl's his watch, thus with his stealthy
   pace,

With Tarquin's ravishing strides, towards his
    design
Moves like a ghost. Thou sure and firm-set
    earth,
Hear not my steps which way they walk, for
    fear
Thy very stones prate of my whereabout,
And take the present horror from the time,
Which now suits with it. Whiles I threat, he
    lives.
Words to the heat of deeds too cold breath
    gives.
    A bell rings
I go, and it is done. The bell invites me.
Hear it not, Duncan; for it is a knell
That summons thee to heaven or to hell.

ACT II: SCENE 2.
   Enter Lady Macbeth

Lady Macbeth: That which hath made them drunk hath made
    me bold,
    What hath quench'd them hath given me fire.
    Hark! Peace! –
    It was the owl that shrieked, the fatal bellman
    Which gives the stern'st good-night. He is
    about it.
    The doors are open, and the surfeited grooms
    Do mock their charge with snores. I have
    drugg'd their possets
    That death and nature do contend about them
    Whether they live or die.
    Enter Macbeth above
Macbeth: Who's there? What ho?
    Exit

Lady Macbeth: Alack! I am afraid they have awaked,
    And 'tis not done. Th' attempt and not the
    deed

Confounds us. Hark! – I laid their daggers
   ready;
He could not miss 'em. Had he not resembled
My father as he slept, I had done't.
Enter Macbeth below

                          My husband!

Macbeth: I have done the deed. Didst thou not hear a
   noise?
Lady Macbeth: I heard the owl scream and the crickets cry.
   Did not you speak?
Macbeth: When?
Lady Macbeth: Now.
Macbeth: As I descended?
Lady Macbeth: Ay.
Macbeth: Hark! – Who lies i'th' second chamber?
Lady Macbeth: Donalbain.
Macbeth: *(looking at his hands)* This is a sorry sight.
Lady Macbeth: A foolish thought, to say a sorry sight.
Macbeth: There's one did laugh in's sleep, and one cried
   'Murder!'
   That they did wake each other. I stood and
   heard them.
   But they did say their prayers, and addressed
   them
   Again to sleep.
Lady Macbeth: There are two lodged together.
Macbeth: One cried 'God bless us!' and 'Amen' the other,
   As they had seen me with these hangman's
   hands.
   List'ning their fear, I could not say 'Amen'
   When they did say 'God bless us.'
Lady Macbeth: Consider it not so deeply.
Macbeth: But wherefore could not I pronounce 'Amen'?
   I had most need of blessing, and 'Amen'
   Stuck in my throat.
Lady Macbeth: These deeds must not be thought
   After these ways. So, it will make us mad.
Macbeth: Methought I heard a voice cry 'Sleep no more,

Macbeth does murder sleep' – the innocent sleep,
Sleep that knits up the ravelled sleave of care,
The death of each day's life, sore labour's bath,
Balm of hurt minds, great nature's second course,
Chief nourisher in life's feast –

Lady Macbeth: What do you mean?

Macbeth: Still it cried 'Sleep no more' to all the house,
'Glamis hath murdered sleep, and therefore Cawdor
Shall sleep no more, Macbeth shall sleep no more!'

Lady Macbeth: Who was it that thus cried? Why, worthy thane,
You do unbend your noble strength to think
So brain-sickly of things. Go get some water
And wash this filthy witness from your hand.
Why did you bring these daggers from the place?
They must lie there. Go, carry them, and smear
The sleepy grooms with blood.

Macbeth: I'll go no more.
I am afraid to think what I have done,
Look on't again I dare not.

Lady Macbeth: Infirm of purpose!
Give me the daggers. The sleeping and the dead
Are but as pictures. 'Tis the eye of childhood
That fears a painted devil. If he do bleed
I'll gild the faces of the grooms withal,
For it must seem their guilt.

Exit

Knock within

Macbeth: Whence is that knocking? –
How is't with me when every noise appals me?
What hands are here! Ha, they pluck out mine eyes.

Will all great Neptune's ocean wash this blood
Clean from my hand? No, this my hand will
   rather
The multitudinous seas incarnadine,
Making the green one red.
   Enter Lady Macbeth

Lady Macbeth: My hands are of your colour, but I shame
To wear a heart so white.
   Knock within

                      I hear a knocking
At the south entry. Retire we to our chamber.
A little water clears us of this deed.
How easy it is then! Your constancy
Hath left you unattended.
   Knock within

                Hark, more knocking.
Get on your nightgown, lest occasion call us
And show us to be watchers. Be not lost
So poorly in your thoughts.

Macbeth: To know my deed 'twere best not know myself.
   Knock within
Wake Duncan with thy knocking. I would thou
   couldst.

ALL SORTS
AND
CONDITIONS
OF MEN

'All human life really is there, with an extraordinary
range and subtlety of characterisation, of historical
setting, of place.'

The Prince of Wales, from his Introduction.

HENRY IV

PART TWO – ACT III: SCENE 2.

Despite his victory at Shrewsbury, an ailing and agitated Henry IV must still deal with rebellion in the north. An army must be levied and Sir John Falstaff, the Prince of Wales's disreputable boon companion, passes through Gloucestershire recruiting men as he goes. Justice Shallow, one of two Justices of the Peace who have assembled men from whom he came make his choice, knew Falstaff in his youth when he was studying at the Inns of Court and he boasts to his cousin, Justice Silence, of madcap exploits which time has greatly exaggerated in his memory.

Shallow:	Come on, come on, come on! Give me your hand, sir, give me your hand, sir. An early stirrer, by the rood! And how doth my good cousin Silence?
Silence:	Good morrow, good cousin Shallow.
Shallow:	And how doth my cousin your bedfellow? And your fairest daughter and mine, my god-daughter Ellen?
Silence:	Alas, a black ouzel, cousin Shallow.
Shallow:	By yea and no, sir, I dare say my cousin William is become a good scholar. He is at Oxford still, is he not?
Silence:	Indeed, sir, to my cost.
Shallow:	A must then to the Inns o' Court shortly. I was once of Clement's Inn, where I think they will talk of mad Shallow yet.
Silence:	You were called 'lusty Shallow' then, cousin.
Shallow:	By the mass, I was called anything; and I would have done anything indeed, too, and roundly, too. There was I, and little John Doit of Staffordshire, and black George Barnes, and Francis Pickbone, and Will Squeal, a Cotswold man; you had not four such swinge-bucklers in all the Inns o' Court again. And I may say to

	you, we knew where the bona-robas were, and had the best of them all at commandment. Then was Jack Falstaff, now Sir John, a boy, and page to Thomas Mowbray, Duke of Norfolk.
Silence:	This Sir John, cousin, that comes hither anon about soldiers?
Shallow:	The same Sir John, the very same. I see him break Scoggin's head at the court gate when a was a crack, not thus high. And the very same day did I fight with one Samson Stockfish, a fruiterer, behind Gray's Inn. Jesu, Jesu, the mad days I have spent! And to see how many of my old acquaintance are dead.
Silence:	We shall all follow, cousin.
Shallow:	Certain, 'tis certain; very sure, very sure. Death, as the Psalmist saith, is certain to all; all shall die. How a good yoke of bullocks at Stamford fair?
Silence:	By my troth, I was not there.
Shallow:	Death is certain. Is old Double of your town living yet?
Silence:	Dead, sir.
Shallow:	Jesu, Jesu, dead! A drew a good bow; and dead! A shot a fine shoot. John o' Gaunt loved him well, and betted much money on his head. Dead! A would have clapped i'th' clout at twelve score, and carried you a forehand shaft a fourteen and fourteen and a half, that it would have done a man's heart good to see. How a score of ewes now?
Silence:	Thereafter as they be. A score of good ewes may be worth ten pounds.
Shallow:	And is old Double dead? . . .
	Enter Sir John Falstaff
Shallow:	. . . Look, here comes good Sir John. *(To Sir John)* Give me your hand, give me your worship's good hand. By my troth, you like

well, and bear your years very well. Welcome, good Sir John.

Sir John: I am glad to see you well, good Master Robert Shallow. . . . Come, I will go drink with you, but I cannot tarry dinner. I am glad to see you, by my troth, Master Shallow.

Shallow: O, Sir John, do you remember since we lay all night in the Windmill in Saint George's Field?

Sir John: No more of that, good Master Shallow, no more of that.

Shallow: Ha, 'twas a merry night! And is Jane Nightwork alive?

Sir John: She lives, Master Shallow.

Shallow: She never could away with me.

Sir John: Never, never. She would always say she could not abide Master Shallow.

Shallow: By the mass, I could anger her to th' heart. She was then a bona-roba. Doth she hold her own well?

Sir John: Old, old, Master Shallow.

Shallow: Nay, she must be old; she cannot choose but be old; certain she's old; and had Robin Nightwork by old Nightwork before I came to Clement's Inn.

Silence: That's fifty-five year ago.

Shallow: Ha, cousin Silence, that thou hadst seen that that this knight and I have seen! Ha, Sir John, said I well?

Sir John: We have heard the chimes at midnight, Master Shallow.

Shallow: That we have, that we have; in faith, Sir John, we have. Our watchword was 'Hem boys!' Come, let's to dinner; come, let's to dinner. Jesus, the days that we have seen! Come, come.

RICHARD III

Act I: Scene 1.

*The House of York has triumphed on the battlefield of Tewkesbury
and Edward IV has been restored to the throne. His younger
brother, Richard, Duke of Gloucester – hunchbacked, ugly and
fitter for violence and stratagem than for the arts of love and peace
– is determined to clear the field of all who stand between him and
the throne. He has begun by persuading Edward to send their
brother Clarence to the throne.*

Richard Gloucester: Now is the winter of our discontent
                Made glorious summer by this son of York;
                And all the clouds that loured upon our house
                In the deep bosom of the ocean buried.
                Now are our brows bound with victorious
                    wreaths,
                Our bruisèd arms hung up for monuments,
                Our stern alarums changed to merry meetings,
                Our dreadful marches to delightful measures.
                Grim-visaged war hath smoothed his wrinkled
                    front,
                And now – instead of mounting barbèd steeds
                To fright the souls of fearful adversaries –
                He capers nimbly in a lady's chamber
                To the lascivious pleasing of a lute.
                But I, that am not shaped for sportive tricks
                Nor made to court an amorous looking-glass,
                I that am rudely stamped and want love's
                    majesty
                To strut before a wanton ambling nymph,
                I that am curtailed of this fair proportion,
                Cheated of feature by dissembling nature,
                Deformed, unfinished, sent before my time
                Into this breathing world scarce half made up –
                And that so lamely and unfashionable
                That dogs bark at me as I halt by them –

Why, I in this weak piping time of peace
Have no delight to pass away the time,
Unless to spy my shadow in the sun
And descant on mine own deformity.
And therefore since I cannot prove a lover
To entertain these fair well-spoken days,
I am determinèd to prove a villain
And hate the idle pleasures of these days.
Plots have I laid, inductions dangerous,
By drunken prophecies, libels and dreams
To set my brother Clarence and the King
In deadly hate the one against the other.
And if King Edward be as true and just
As I am subtle false and treacherous,
This day should Clarence closely be mewed up
About a prophecy which says that 'G'
Of Edward's heirs the murderer shall be.

*Enter George Duke of Clarence, guarded, and
Sir Robert Brackenbury*

Dive, thoughts, down to my soul: here
Clarence comes.

THE WINTER'S TALE

ACT III: SCENE 3.

*Leontes, the Sicilian King, has conceived an unreasoning jealousy
of his wife, Hermione, and he suspects that her new-born baby
daughter was in fact fathered by his old friend Polixenes, the King
of Bohemia. Consequently he sends Antigonus, one of his courtiers,
on the perilous sea voyage to Bohemia with instructions to abandon
the infant in some remote place. A violent storm is brewing as
Antigonus is landed on the shore and straight into the middle of a
bear-hunt. He leaves both baby and her accompanying box of gold
on the sand and takes to his heels when the bear comes lumbering
towards him. Antigonus is devoured while his ship founders in the
storm and sinks with all hands. An old shepherd and his bumpkin
son discover the baby and so Perdita – the lost child – is taken to
her new home, to be raised as a shepherdess.*

Old Shepherd: I would there were no age between ten and
three-and-twenty, or that youth would sleep
out the rest; for there is nothing in the between
but getting wenches with child, wronging the
ancientry, stealing, fighting – hark you now,
would any but these boiled-brains of nineteen
and two-and-twenty hunt this weather? They
have scared away two of my best sheep, which
I fear the wolf will sooner find than the master.
If anywhere I have them, 'tis by the seaside,
browsing of ivy. Good luck, an't be thy will!
  He sees the babe
What have we here? Mercy on's, a bairn! A
very pretty bairn. A boy or a child, I wonder? A
pretty one, a very pretty one. Sure some scape.
Though I am not bookish, yet I can read
'waiting-gentlewoman' in the scape. This has
been some stair-work, some trunk-work, some
behind-door-work. They were warmer that got
this than the poor thing is here. I'll take it up

for pity; yet I'll tarry till my son come. He
hallooed but even now. Whoa-ho-hoa!
Enter Clown

Clown: Hilloa, loa!

Old Shepherd: What, art so near? If thou'lt see a thing to talk
on when thou art dead and rotten, come hither.
What ail'st thou, man?

Clown: I have seen two such sights, by sea and by
land! But I am not to say it is a sea, for it is now
the sky. Betwixt the firmament and it you
cannot thrust a bodkin's point.

Old Shepherd: Why, boy, how is it?

Clown: I would you did but see how it chafes, how it
rages, how it takes up the shore. But that's not
to the point. O, the most piteous cry of the
poor souls! Sometimes to see 'em, and not to
see 'em; now the ship boring the moon with
her mainmast, and anon swallowed with yeast
and froth, as you'd thrust a cork into a
hogshead. And then for the land-service, to see
how the bear tore out his shoulder-bone, how
he cried to me for help, and said his name was
Antigonus, a nobleman! But to make an end of
the ship – to see how the sea flap-dragoned it!
But first, how the poor souls roared, and the
sea mocked them, and how the poor gentleman
roared, and the bear mocked him, both roaring
louder than the sea or weather.

Old Shepherd: Name of mercy, when was this, boy?

Clown: Now, now. I have not winked since I saw these
sights. The men are not yet cold under water,
nor the bear half dined on the gentleman. He's
at it now.

Old Shepherd: Would I had been by to have helped the old
man!

Clown: I would you had been by the ship side, to have
helped her. There your charity would have
lacked footing.

Old Shepherd: Heavy matters, heavy matters. But look thee here, boy. Now bless thyself. Thou metst with things dying, I with things new-born. Here's a sight for thee. Look thee, a bearing-cloth for a squire's child.

> *He points to the box*

Look thee here, take up, take up, boy. Open't. So, let's see. It was told me I should be rich by the fairies. This is some changeling. Open't. What's within, boy?

Clown: *(opening the box)* You're a made old man. If the sins of your youth are forgiven you, you're well to live. Gold, all gold!

Old Shepherd: This is fairy gold, boy, and 'twill prove so. Up with't, keep it close. Home, home, the next way. We are lucky, boy, and to be so still requires nothing but secrecy. Let my sheep go. Come, good boy, the next way home.

Clown: Go you the next way with your findings. I'll go see if the bear be gone from the gentleman, and how much he hath eaten. They are never curst but when they are hungry. If there be any of him left, I'll bury it.

Old Shepherd: That's a good deed. If thou mayst discern by that which is left of him what he is, fetch me to th' sight of him.

Clown: Marry will I: and you shall help to put him i'th' ground.

Old Shepherd: 'Tis a lucky day, boy, and we'll do good deeds on't.

THE MERCHANT OF VENICE

ACT III: SCENE 1.

*Shylock the Jew is devastated by the loss of his only child, Jessica,
who has eloped with the young Venetian, Lorenzo, who is a
Christian. As it happens Shylock has obliged Antonio, the
Venetian merchant whom he most dislikes, with a loan. In what he
pretends is 'merry sport' he has lent the money on condition that if
it is not repaid the forfeit will be a pound of Antonio's flesh. When
several of Antonio's ships are lost at sea and the payment is
becoming due, most people think that the Jew will not exact his
pound of flesh. Shylock, who has suffered at the hands of Antonio
and other Christians for no reason other than that he is a Jew,
disabuses them.*

Shylock: I am a Jew. Hath not a Jew eyes? Hath not a
Jew hands, organs, dimensions, senses,
affections, passions; fed with the same food,
hurt with the same weapons, subject to the
same diseases, healed by the same means,
warmed and cooled by the same winter and
summer as a Christian is? If you prick us do we
not bleed? If you tickle us do we not laugh? If
you poison us do we not die? And if you wrong
us shall we not revenge? If we are like you in
the rest, we will resemble you in that. If a Jew
wrong a Christian, what is his humility?
Revenge. If a Christian wrong a Jew, what
should his sufferance be by Christian example?
Why, revenge. The villainy you teach me I will
execute, and it shall go hard but I will better the
instruction.

JULIUS CAESAR

Act IV: Scene 2.

*Julius Caesar has been assassinated; the power of Mark Antony's
oratory has inflamed the populace, and the conspirators have been
forced to flee from Rome. Brutus and Cassius, the leaders of the
conspiracy against Caesar, each raise armies to do battle with the
forces of Mark Antony and Octavius at Philippi. As soon as they
meet in camp at Sardis there is dissension between them. Brutus,
famed for his integrity, has charged one of Cassius's lieutenants
with corruption and accuses Cassius of supporting him. Cassius
flies into a rage and hot-tempered insults are exchanged before
Cassius dramatically wins back Brutus's friendship.*

Cassius:	That you have wronged me doth appear in this:
	You have condemned and noted Lucius Pella
	For taking bribes here of the Sardians,
	Wherein my letters praying on his side,
	Because I knew the man, was slighted off.
Brutus:	You wronged yourself to write in such a case.
Cassius:	In such a time as this it is not meet
	That every nice offence should bear his
	comment.
Brutus:	Let me tell you, Cassius, you yourself
	Are much condemned to have an itching palm,
	To sell and mart your offices for gold
	To undeservers.
Cassius:	I, an itching palm?
	You know that you are Brutus that speaks this,
	Or, by the gods, this speech were else your
	last. . . .
Brutus:	You have done that you should be sorry for.
	There is no terror, Cassius, in your threats,
	For I am armed so strong in honesty
	That they pass by me as the idle wind,
	Which I respect not. I did send to you
	For certain sums of gold, which you denied me;

For I can raise no money by vile means.
By heaven, I had rather coin my heart
And drop my blood for drachmas than to wring
From the hard hands of peasants their vile
     trash
By any indirection. I did send
To you for gold to pay my legions,
Which you denied me. Was that done like
     Cassius?
Should I have answered Caius Cassius so?
When Marcus Brutus grows so covetous
To lock such rascal counters from his friends,
Be ready, gods, with all your thunderbolts;
Dash him to pieces.

Cassius:	I denied you not.
Brutus:	You did.
Cassius:	I did not. He was but a fool

That brought my answer back. Brutus hath
     rived my heart.
A friend should bear his friend's infirmities,
But Brutus makes mine greater than they are.

Brutus:	I do not, till you practise them on me.
Cassius:	You love me not.
Brutus:	I do not like your faults.
Cassius:	A friendly eye could never see such faults.
Brutus:	A flatterer's would not, though they do appear

As huge as high Olympus.

Cassius: Come, Antony and young Octavius, come,
Revenge yourselves alone on Cassius;
For Cassius is aweary of the world,
Hated by one he loves, braved by his brother,
Checked like a bondman; all his faults
     observed,
Set in a notebook, learned and conned by rote,
To cast into my teeth. O, I could weep
My spirit from mine eyes! There is my dagger,
And here my naked breast; within, a heart
Dearer than Pluto's mine, richer than gold.

If that thou beest a Roman, take it forth.
I that denied thee gold will give my heart.
Strike as thou didst at Caesar; for I know
When thou didst hate him worst, thou loved'st
    him better
Than ever thou loved'st Cassius.

Brutus: Sheathe your dagger.
Be angry when you will; it shall have scope.
Do what you will; dishonour shall be humour.
O Cassius, you are yokèd with a lamb
That carries anger as the flint bears fire,
Who, much enforcèd, shows a hasty spark
And straight is cold again.

Cassius: Hath Cassius lived
To be both mirth and laughter to his Brutus
When grief and blood ill-tempered vexeth him?

Brutus: When I spoke that, I was ill-tempered too.
Cassius: Do you confess so much? Give me your hand.
Brutus: And my heart too.

HUMOUR

'That you can have fun with Shakespeare seems to me to be something which each generation has to discover anew for itself.'

The Prince of Wales, from his Introduction.

MUCH ADO ABOUT NOTHING

Act I: Scene 1.

Don Pedro, Prince of Aragon, arrives in Messina with his captains Benedick and Claudio after crushing the revolt of his half-brother Don John. Leonato, Governor of the city, invites them to stay for some days of merry-making. While Claudio is drawn to Leonato's daughter Hero, Benedick crosses verbal swords once again with his old adversary, her sharp-tongued cousin, Beatrice.

Beatrice:	I pray you, is Signor Montanto returned from the wars, or no?
Messenger:	I know none of that name, lady. There was none such in the army, of any sort.
Leonato:	What is he that you ask for, niece?
Hero:	My cousin means Signor Benedick of Padua.
Messenger:	O, he's returned, and as pleasant as ever he was.
Beatrice:	He set up his bills here in Messina, and challenged Cupid at the flight; and my uncle's fool, reading the challenge, subscribed for Cupid and challenged him at the bird-bolt. I pray you, how many hath he killed and eaten in these wars? But how many hath he killed? For indeed I promised to eat all of his killing.
Leonato:	Faith, niece, you tax Signor Benedick too much. But he'll meet with you, I doubt it not.
Messenger:	He hath done good service, lady, in these wars.
Beatrice:	You had musty victual, and he hath holp to eat it. He is a very valiant trencherman, he hath an excellent stomach.
Messenger:	And a good soldier too, lady.
Beatrice:	And a good soldier to a lady, but what is he to a lord?
Messenger:	A lord to a lord, a man to a man, stuffed with all honourable virtues.

Beatrice:	It is so, indeed. He is no less than a stuffed man. But for the stuffing – well, we are all mortal.
Leonato:	You must not, sir, mistake my niece. There is a kind of merry war betwixt Signor Benedick and her. They never meet but there's a skirmish of wit between them.
Beatrice:	Alas, he gets nothing by that. In our last conflict four of his five wits went halting off, and now is the whole man governed with one, so that if he have wit enough to keep himself warm, let him bear it for a difference between himself and his horse, for it is all the wealth that he hath left to be known a reasonable creature. Who is his companion now? He hath every month a new sworn brother.
Messenger:	Is't possible?
Beatrice:	Very easily possible. He wears his faith but as the fashion of his hat, it ever changes with the next block.
Messenger:	I see, lady, the gentleman is not in your books.
Beatrice:	No. An he were, I would burn my study. But I pray you, who is his companion? Is there no young squarer now that will make a voyage with him to the devil?
Messenger:	He is most in the company of the right noble Claudio.
Beatrice:	O Lord, he will hang upon him like a disease. He is sooner caught than the pestilence, and the taker runs presently mad. God help the noble Claudio. If he have caught the Benedick, it will cost him a thousand pound ere a be cured.
Messenger:	I will hold friends with you, lady.
Beatrice:	Do, good friend.
Leonato:	You will never run mad, niece.
Beatrice:	No, not till a hot January.

Messenger:	Don Pedro is approached.
	Enter Don Pedro, Claudio, Benedick, Balthasar,
	and Don John the bastard
Don Pedro:	Good Signor Leonato, are you come to meet
	your trouble? The fashion of the world is to
	avoid cost, and you encounter it.
Leonato:	Never came trouble to my house in the likeness
	of your grace; for trouble being gone, comfort
	should remain, but when you depart from me,
	sorrow abides and happiness takes his leave.
Don Pedro:	You embrace your charge too willingly. I think
	this is your daughter.
Leonato:	Her mother hath many times told me so.
Benedick:	Were you in doubt, sir, that you asked her?
Leonato:	Signor Benedick, no, for then were you a
	child.
Don Pedro:	You have it full, Benedick. We may guess by
	this what you are, being a man. Truly, the lady
	fathers herself. Be happy, lady, for you are like
	an honourable father.
Benedick:	If Signor Leonato be her father, she would not
	have his head on her shoulders for all Messina,
	as like him as she is.
Beatrice:	I wonder that you will still be talking, Signor
	Benedick. Nobody marks you.
Benedick:	What, my dear Lady Disdain! Are you yet
	living?
Beatrice:	Is it possible disdain should die while she hath
	such meet food to feed it as Signor Benedick?
	Courtesy itself must convert to disdain if you
	come in her presence.
Benedick:	Then is courtesy a turncoat. But it is certain I
	am loved of all ladies, only you excepted. And I
	would I could find in my heart that I had not a
	hard heart, for truly I love none.
Beatrice:	A dear happiness to women. They would else
	have been troubled with a pernicious suitor. I
	thank God and my cold blood I am of your

	humour for that. I had rather hear my dog bark at a crow than a man swear he loves me.
Benedick:	God keep your ladyship still in that mind. So some gentleman or other shall scape a predestinate scratched face.
Beatrice:	Scratching could not make it worse an 'twere such a face as yours were.
Benedick:	Well, you are a rare parrot-teacher.
Beatrice:	A bird of my tongue is better than a beast of yours.
Benedick:	I would my horse had the speed of your tongue, and so good a continuer. But keep your way, o' God's name. I have done.
Beatrice:	You always end with a jade's trick. I know you of old.

MUCH ADO ABOUT NOTHING

ACT IV: SCENE 1.

To the anger and consternation of her family and friends, Hero has been publicly humiliated at the altar, falsely accused of immorality by her bridegroom, Claudio. When the wedding party breaks up in confusion, Beatrice and Benedick are left alone and Benedick at last declares his love for her. Beatrice demands as proof of his love that he should take vengeance on Claudio for the way he has treated her cousin.

Benedick:	Lady Beatrice, have you wept all this while?
Beatrice:	Yea, and I will weep a while longer.
Benedick:	I will not desire that.
Beatrice:	You have no reason, I do it freely.
Benedick:	Surely I do believe your fair cousin is wronged.
Beatrice:	Ah, how much might the man deserve of me that would right her!
Benedick:	Is there any way to show such friendship?
Beatrice:	A very even way, but no such friend.
Benedick:	May a man do it?
Beatrice:	It is a man's office, but not yours.
Benedick:	I do love nothing in the world so well as you. Is not that strange?
Beatrice:	As strange as the thing I know not. It were as possible for me to say I loved nothing so well as you, but believe me not, and yet I lie not. I confess nothing nor I deny nothing. I am sorry for my cousin.
Benedick:	By my sword, Beatrice, thou lovest me.
Beatrice:	Do not swear and eat it.
Benedick:	I will swear by it that you love me, and I will make him eat it that says I love not you.
Beatrice:	Will you not eat your word?
Benedick:	With no sauce that can be devised to it. I protest I love thee.
Beatrice:	Why then, God forgive me.

Benedick:	What offence, sweet Beatrice?
Beatrice:	You have stayed me in a happy hour. I was about to protest I loved you.
Benedick:	And do it with all thy heart.
Beatrice:	I love you with so much of my heart that none is left to protest.
Benedick:	Come, bid me do anything for thee.
Beatrice:	Kill Claudio.
Benedick:	Ha! Not for the wide world.
Beatrice:	You kill me to deny it. Farewell.
Benedick:	Tarry, sweet Beatrice.
Beatrice:	I am gone though I am here. There is no love in you. – Nay, I pray you, let me go.
Benedick:	Beatrice.
Beatrice:	In faith, I will go.
Benedick:	We'll be friends first.
Beatrice:	You dare easier be friends with me than fight with mine enemy.
Benedick:	Is Claudio thine enemy?
Beatrice:	Is a not approved in the height a villain, that hath slandered, scorned, dishonoured my kinswoman? O that I were a man! What, bear her in hand until they come to take hands, and then with public accusation, uncovered slander, unmitigated rancour – O God that I were a man! I would eat his heart in the market place.
Benedick:	Hear me, Beatrice.
Beatrice:	Talk with a man out at a window – a proper saying!
Benedick:	Nay, but Beatrice.
Beatrice:	Sweet Hero, she is wronged, she is slandered, she is undone.
Benedick:	Beat—
Beatrice:	Princes and counties! Surely a princely testimony, a goodly count, Count Comfit, a sweet gallant, surely. O that I were a man for his sake! Or that I had any friend would be a

man for my sake! But manhood is melted into courtesies, valour into compliment, and men are only turned into tongue, and trim ones, too. He is now as valiant as Hercules that only tells a lie and swears it. I cannot be a man with wishing, therefore I will die a woman with grieving.

Benedick: Tarry, good Beatrice. By this hand, I love thee.

Beatrice: Use it for my love some other way than swearing by it.

Benedick: Think you in your soul the Count Claudio hath wronged Hero?

Beatrice: Yea, as sure as I have a thought or a soul.

Benedick: Enough, I am engaged, I will challenge him. I will kiss your hand, and so I leave you. By this hand, Claudio shall render me a dear account. As you hear of me, so think of me. Go comfort your cousin. I must say she is dead. And so, farewell.

MACBETH

ACT II: SCENE 3.

It is morning. Macduff arrives at the gate of Macbeth's castle to attend on the King, and has difficulty arousing the Porter from his drunken slumber. No-one has yet discovered that King Duncan lies slaughtered in his bed, but ironically the Porter pretends for a few moments that he is opening the gates of Hell.

Porter: Here's a knocking indeed! If a man were porter of hell-gate he should have old turning the key.

                Knock within

            Knock, knock, knock. Who's there, i'th' name of Beelzebub? Here's a farmer that hanged himself on th' expectation of plenty. Come in time! Have napkins enough about you; here you'll sweat for't.

                Knock within

            Knock, knock. Who's there, in th' other devil's name? Faith, here's an equivocator that could swear in both the scales against either scale, who committed treason enough for God's sake, yet could not equivocate to heaven. O, come in, equivocator.

                Knock within

            Knock, knock, knock. Who's there? 'Faith, here's an English tailor come hither for stealing out of a French hose. Come in, tailor. Here you may roast your goose.

                Knock within

            Knock, knock. Never at quiet. What are you? – But this place is too cold for hell. I'll devil-porter it no further. I had thought to have let in some of all professions that go the primrose way to th' everlasting bonfire.

                Knock within

Anon, anon!
He opens the gate
I pay you remember the porter.
Enter Macduff and Lennox

Macduff: Was it so late, friend, ere you went to bed
That you do lie so late?

Porter: Faith, sir, we were carousing till the second cock, and drink, sir, is a great provoker of three things.

Macduff: What three things does drink especially provoke?

Porter: Marry, sir, nose-painting, sleep, and urine. Lechery, sir, it provokes and unprovokes: it provokes the desire but it takes away the performance. Therefore much drink may be said to be an equivocator with lechery: it makes him and it mars him; it sets him on and it takes him off; it persuades him and disheartens him, makes him stand to and not stand to; in conclusion, equivocates him in a sleep, and, giving him the lie, leaves him.

Macduff: I believe drink gave thee the lie last night.

Porter: That it did, sir, i'the very throat on me; but I requited him for his lie, and, I think, being too strong for him, though he took up my legs sometime, yet I made a shift to cast him.

TWELFTH NIGHT

The overbearing airs and sanctimonious officiousness of Olivia's steward, Malvolio, have so incensed the other members of her household that they have laid a trap for him. Maria, Olivia's lady-in-waiting, has dropped a letter, apparently in her mistress's hand-writing, where Malvolio is likely to find it. Malvolio strolls into the garden, enjoying himself with delicious fantasies of what life would be like were Olivia to reveal what he believes to be a secret passion for him and so make him master. Such imaginings cause outbursts of spluttering rage from his chief enemy Sir Toby Belch, Olivia's roistering uncle, who is concealed in the garden with his confederates, Sir Andrew Aguecheek and the servant, Fabian. To the delight of his unseen audience, Malvolio discovers the letter, which seems to embody all his most intimate hopes, and he swallows the bait whole.

Malvolio:	'Tis but fortune, all is fortune. Maria once told me she did affect me, and I have heard herself come thus near, that should she fancy it should be one of my complexion. Besides, she uses me with a more exalted respect than anyone else that follows her. What should I think on't?
Sir Toby:	Here's an overweening rogue.
Fabian:	O, peace! Contemplation makes a rare turkeycock of him – how he jets under his advanced plumes!
Sir Andrew:	'Slight, I could so beat the rogue.
Sir Toby:	Peace, I say.
Malvolio:	Ah, rogue.
Sir Andrew:	Pistol him, pistol him.
Sir Toby:	Peace, peace.
Malvolio:	There is example for't: the Lady of the Strachey married the yeoman of the wardrobe.
Sir Andrew:	Fie on him, Jezebel.

Fabian:	O peace, now he's deeply in. Look how imagination blows him.
Malvolio:	Having been three months married to her, sitting in my state –
Sir Toby:	O for a stone-bow to hit him in the eye!
Malvolio:	Calling my officers about me, in my branched velvet gown, having come from a day-bed where I have left Olivia sleeping –
Sir Toby:	Fire and brimstone!
Fabian:	O peace, peace.
Malvolio:	And then to have the humour of state and – after a demure travel of regard, telling them I know my place, as I would they should do theirs – to ask for my kinsman Toby.
Sir Toby:	Bolts and shackles!
Fabian:	O peace, peace, peace, now, now.
Malvolio:	Seven of my people with an obedient start make out for him. I frown the while, and perchance wind up my watch, or play with my – *(touching his chain)* some rich jewel. Toby approaches; curtsies there to me.
Sir Toby:	Shall this fellow live?
Fabian:	Though our silence be drawn from us with cars, yet peace.
Malvolio:	I extend my hand to him thus, quenching my familiar smile with an austere regard of control –
Sir Toby:	And does not Toby take you a blow o' the lips, then?
Malvolio:	Saying 'Cousin Toby, my fortunes, having cast me on your niece, give me this prerogative of speech' –
Sir Toby:	What, what!
Malvolio:	'You must amend your drunkenness.'
Sir Toby:	Out, scab.
Fabian:	Nay, patience, or we break the sinews of our plot.
Malvolio:	'Besides, you waste the treasure of your time with a foolish knight' –

Sir Andrew:	That's me, I warrant you.
Malvolio:	'One Sir Andrew.'
Sir Andrew:	I knew 'twas I, for many do call me fool.
Malvolio:	*(seeing the letter)* What employment have we here?
Fabian:	Now is the woodcock near the gin.
Sir Toby:	O peace, and the spirit of humours intimate reading aloud to him.
Malvolio:	*(taking up the letter)* By my life, this is my lady's hand. These be her very c's, her u's, and her t's, and thus makes she her great P's. It is in contempt of question her hand.
Sir Andrew:	Her c's, her u's, and her t's? Why that?
Malvolio:	*(reads)* 'To the unknown beloved, this, and my good wishes.' Her very phrases! *(opening the letter)* By your leave, wax – soft, and the impressure her Lucrece, with which she uses to seal – 'tis my lady. To whom should this be?
Fabian:	This wins him, liver and all.
Malvolio:	'Jove knows I love, But who? Lips do not move, No man must know.' 'No man must know.' What follows? The number's altered. 'No man must know.' If this should be thee, Malvolio?
Sir Toby:	Marry, hang thee, brock.
Malvolio:	'I may command where I adore, But silence like a Lucrece knife With bloodless stroke my heart doth gore. M.O.A.I. doth sway my life.'
Fabian:	A fustian riddle.
Sir Toby:	Excellent wench, say I.
Malvolio:	'M.O.A.I. doth sway my life.' Nay, but first let me see, let me see, let me see.
Fabian:	What dish o' poison has she dressed him!
Sir Toby:	And with what wing the staniel checks at it!
Malvolio:	'I may command where I adore.' Why, she may

command me. I serve her, she is my lady.
Why, this is evident to any formal capacity.
There is no obstruction in this. And the end –
what should that alphabetical position portend?
If I could make that resemble something in me.
Softly – 'M.O.A.I.'

Sir Toby: O ay, make up that, he is now at a cold scent.

Fabian: Sowter will cry upon't for all this, though it be
as rank as a fox.

Malvolio: 'M.' Malvolio – 'M' – why, that begins my
name.

Fabian: Did not I say he would work it out? The cur is
excellent at faults.

Malvolio: 'M.' But then there is no consonancy in the
sequel. That suffers under probation. 'A'
should follow, but 'O' does.

Fabian: And 'O' shall end, I hope.

Sir Toby: Ay, or I'll cudgel him, and make him cry 'O!'

Malvolio: And then 'I' comes behind.

Fabian: Ay, an you had any eye behind you you might
see more detraction at your heels than fortune
before you.

Malvolio: 'M.O.A.I.' This simulation is not as the former;
and yet to crush this a little, it would bow to
me, for every one of these letters are in my
name. Soft, here follows prose: 'If this fall into
thy hand, revolve. In my stars I am above thee,
but be not afraid of greatness. Some are born
great, some achieve greatness, and some have
greatness thrust upon 'em. Thy fates open their
hands, let thy blood and spirit embrace them,
and to inure thyself to what thou art like to be,
cast thy humble slough, and appear fresh. Be
opposite with a kinsman, surly with servants.
Let thy tongue tang arguments of state; put
thyself into the trick of singularity. She thus
advises thee that sighs for thee. Remember
who commended thy yellow stockings, and

wished to see thee ever cross-gartered. I say remember, go to, thou art made if thou desirest to be so; if not, let me see thee a steward still, the fellow of servants, and not worthy to touch Fortune's fingers. Farewell. She that would alter services with thee,

The Fortunate-Unhappy.'
Daylight and champaign discovers not more. This is open. I will be proud, I will read politic authors, I will baffle Sir Toby, I will wash off gross acquaintance, I will be point-device the very man. I do not now fool myself, to let imagination jade me; for every reason excites to this, that my lady loves me. She did commend my yellow stockings of late, she did praise my leg, being cross-gartered, and in this she manifests herself to my love, and with a kind of injunction drives me to these habits of her liking. I thank my stars, I am happy. I will be strange, stout, in yellow stockings, and cross-gartered, even with the swiftness of putting on. Jove and my stars be praised. Here is yet a postscript. 'Thou canst not choose but know who I am. If thou entertainest my love, let it appear in thy smiling, thy smiles become thee well. Therefore in my presence still smile, dear my sweet, I prithee.' Jove, I thank thee. I will smile, I will do everything that thou wilt have me.

THE
DARKER
SIDE

'How do we teach people to recognise that there is a dark side too to man's psyche and that its destructive power is immense if we are not aware of it?'

The Prince of Wales, speech at the 350th anniversary of Harvard University, 1986.

'There is Good and there is Evil. There is Death and there is also Life. The fact that we have had no major war in Europe for fifty years . . . does not mean that modern man has somehow conquered the dark side of our human condition which always lurks, menacingly, in the shadows.'

The Prince of Wales, 'Thought for the Day', VE Day anniversary, 1995.

HAMLET

The ghost of Hamlet's father has revealed to his son that his recent death was murder and that the murderer was Claudius, Hamlet's detested uncle, who has now taken the throne of Denmark and married the widowed Queen. Aware that he must avenge his father's death, yet plunged in debilitating despair, Hamlet reflects, in the most famous of all Shakespearean soliloquies, on the temptation of suicide as a solution to the anguish of life.

Hamlet: To be, or not to be; that is the question:
Whether 'tis nobler in the mind to suffer
The slings and arrows of outrageous fortune,
Or to take arms against a sea of troubles,
And, by opposing, end them. To die, to sleep –
No more, and by a sleep to say we end
The heartache and the thousand natural shocks
That flesh is heir to – 'tis a consummation
Devoutly to be wished. To die, to sleep.
To sleep, perchance to dream. Ay, there's the
    rub,
For in that sleep of death what dreams may
    come
When we have shuffled off this mortal coil
Must give us pause. There's the respect
That makes calamity of so long life,
For who would bear the whips and scorns of
    time,
Th' oppressor's wrong, the proud man's
    contumely,
The pangs of disprized love, the law's delay,
The insolence of office, and the spurns
That patient merit of th' unworthy takes,
When he himself might his quietus make
With a bare bodkin? Who would these fardels
    bear,

To grunt and sweat under a weary life,
But that the dread of something after death,
The undiscovered country from whose bourn
No traveller returns, puzzles the will,
And makes us rather bear those ills we have
Than fly to others that we know not of?
Thus conscience does make cowards of us all,
And thus the native hue of resolution
Is sicklied o'er with the pale cast of thought,
And enterprises of great pith and moment
With this regard their currents turn awry,
And lose the name of action.

HAMLET

ACT II: SCENE 2.

To help him conceal his true feelings while he plans his revenge on Claudius, Hamlet has feigned madness. Worried by his nephew's erratic behaviour, the King summons Rosencrantz and Guildenstern, old school-fellows of the Prince, and asks them to find out what is wrong with him. Quickly realising that they have come to spy on him, Hamlet offers them an analysis of his state of mind – a kind of dark depression which takes all pleasure from the world and paints human existence in sombre hues.

Hamlet: I have of late – but wherefore I know not – lost all my mirth, forgone all custom of exercise; and indeed it goes so heavily with my disposition that this goodly frame, the earth, seems to me a sterile promontory. This most excellent canopy the air, look you, this brave o'erhanging, this majestical roof fretted with golden fire – why, it appears no other thing to me than a foul and pestilent congregation of vapours. What a piece of work is a man! How noble in reason, how infinite in faculty, in form and moving how express and admirable, in action how like an angel, in apprehension how like a god – the beauty of the world, the paragon of animals! And yet to me what is this quintessence of dust? Man delights not me – no, nor woman neither, though by your smiling you seem to say so.

OTHELLO

ACT III: SCENE 3.

*Furious that he has been passed over in favour of Cassio for the
position of Othello's lieutenant, Iago has engineered a drunken
brawl which brings about the disgrace and demotion of his rival.
Partly for sheer devilry, partly because he suspects that Othello
may have been intimate with his own wife Emilia, Iago sets out
next to destroy the happiness of Othello's marriage with
Desdemona. Her innocently open-hearted espousal of Cassio's
campaign to win back Othello's favour provides the perfect
opportunity for Iago's poisonous innuendo.*

Othello:	What dost thou say, Iago?
Iago:	Did Michael Cassio, when you wooed my lady, Know of your love?
Othello:	He did, from first to last. Why dost thou ask?
Iago:	But for a satisfaction of my thought, No further harm.
Othello:	Why of thy thought, Iago?
Iago:	I did not think he had been acquainted with her.
Othello:	O yes, and went between us very oft.
Iago:	Indeed?
Othello:	Indeed? Ay, indeed. Discern'st thou aught in that? Is he not honest?
Iago:	Honest, my lord?
Othello:	Honest? Ay, honest.
Iago:	My lord, for aught I know.
Othello:	What dost thou think?
Iago:	Think, my lord?
Othello:	'Think, my lord?' By heaven, thou echo'st me As if there were some monster in thy thought Too hideous to be shown! Thou dost mean something. I heard thee say even now thou liked'st not that,

When Cassio left my wife. What didst not like?
And when I told thee he was of my counsel
In my whole course of wooing, thou cried'st
    'Indeed?'
And didst contract and purse thy brow together
As if thou then hadst shut up in thy brain
Some horrible conceit. If thou dost love me,
Show me thy thought.

Iago: My lord, you know I love you.
Othello: I think thou dost,
And for I know thou'rt full of love and honesty,
And weigh'st thy words before thou giv'st
    them breath,
Therefore these stops of thine fright me the
    more;
For such things in a false disloyal knave
Are tricks of custom, but in a man that's just,
They're close dilations, working from the heart
That passion cannot rule.

Iago: For Michael Cassio,
I dare be sworn I think that he is honest.
Othello: I think so too.
Iago: Men should be what they seem,
Or those that be not, would they might seem
    none.
Othello: Certain, men should be what they seem.
Iago: Why then, I think Cassio's an honest man.
Othello: Nay, yet there's more in this.
I prithee speak to me as to thy thinkings,
As thou dost ruminate, and give thy worst of
    thoughts
The worst of words.
Iago: Good my lord, pardon me.
Though I am bound to every act of duty,
I am not bound to that all slaves are free to.
Utter my thoughts? Why, say they are vile and
    false,
As where's that palace whereinto foul things

Sometimes intrude not? Who has that breast so pure
But some uncleanly apprehensions
Keep leets and law-days, and in sessions sit
With meditations lawful?

Othello: Thou dost conspire against thy friend, Iago,
If thou but think'st him wronged and mak'st his ear
A stranger to thy thoughts.

Iago: I do beseech you,
Though I perchance am vicious in my guess –
As I confess it is my nature's plague
To spy into abuses, and oft my jealousy
Shapes faults that are not – that your wisdom then,
From one that so imperfectly conceits,
Would take no notice, nor build yourself a trouble
Out of his scattering and unsure observance.
It were not for your quiet nor your good,
Nor for my manhood, honesty, and wisdom,
To let you know my thoughts.

Othello: What dost thou mean?

Iago: Good name in man and woman, dear my lord,
Is the immediate jewel of their souls.
Who steals my purse steals trash; 'tis something, nothing;
'Twas mine, 'tis his, and has been slave to thousands.
But he that filches from me my good name
Robs me of that which not enriches him
And makes me poor indeed.

Othello: By heaven, I'll know thy thoughts.

Iago: You cannot, if my heart were in your hand;
Nor shall not whilst 'tis in my custody.

Othello: Ha!

Iago: O, beware, my lord, of jealousy.
It is the green-eyed monster which doth mock

The meat it feeds on. That cuckold lives in bliss
Who, certain of his fate, loves not his wronger.
But O, what damnèd minutes tells he o'er
Who dotes yet doubts, suspects yet fondly
    loves!

Othello: O misery!

Iago: Poor and content is rich, and rich enough,
But riches fineless is as poor as winter
To him that ever fears he shall be poor.
Good God the souls of all my tribe defend
From jealousy!

Othello: Why, why is this?
Think'st thou I'd make a life of jealousy,
To follow still the changes of the moon
With fresh suspicions? No, to be once in doubt
Is once to be resolved. Exchange me for a goat
When I shall turn the business of my soul
To such exsufflicate and blowed surmises
Matching thy inference. 'Tis not to make me
    jealous
To say my wife is fair, feeds well, loves
    company,
Is free of speech, sings, plays, and dances well.
Where virtue is, these are more virtuous,
Nor from mine own weak merits will I draw
The smallest fear or doubt of her revolt,
For she had eyes and chose me. No, Iago,
I'll see before I doubt; when I doubt, prove;
And on the proof, there is no more but this:
Away at once with love or jealousy.

Iago: I am glad of this, for now I shall have reason
To show the love and duty that I bear you
With franker spirit. Therefore, as I am bound,
Receive it from me. I speak not yet of proof.
Look to your wife. Observe her well with
    Cassio.
Wear your eyes thus: not jealous, nor secure.
I would not have your free and noble nature

Out of self-bounty be abused. Look to't.
I know our country disposition well.
In Venice they do let God see the pranks
They dare not show their husbands; their best conscience
Is not to leave't undone, but keep't unknown.

Othello: Dost thou say so?

Iago: She did deceive her father, marrying you,
And when she seemed to shake and fear your looks
She loved them most.

Othello: And so she did.

Iago: Why, go to, then.
She that so young could give out such a seeming,
To seel her father's eyes up close as oak,
He thought 'twas witchcraft! But I am much to blame.
I humbly beseech you of your pardon
For too much loving you.

Othello: I am bound to thee for ever.

Iago: I see this hath a little dashed your spirits.

Othello: Not a jot, not a jot.

Iago: I'faith, I fear it has.
I hope you will consider what is spoke
Comes from my love. But I see you're moved.
I am to pray you not to strain my speech
To grosser issues, nor to larger reach
Than to suspicion.

Othello: I will not.

Iago: Should you do so, my lord,
My speech should fall into such vile success
Which my thoughts aimed not. Cassio's my worthy friend.
My lord, I see you're moved.

Othello: No, not much moved.
I do not think but Desdemona's honest.

Iago: Long live she so, and long live you to think so!

Othello:	And yet how nature, erring from itself –
Iago:	Ay, there's the point; as, to be bold with you,
	Not to affect many proposèd matches
	Of her own clime, complexion, and degree,
	Whereto we see in all things nature tends.
	Foh, one may smell in such a will most rank,
	Foul disproportions, thoughts unnatural!
	But pardon me. I do not in position
	Distinctly speak of her, though I may fear
	Her will, recoiling to her better judgement,
	May fall to match you with her country forms
	And happily repent.
Othello:	Farewell, farewell.
	If more thou dost perceive, let me know more.
	Set on thy wife to observe. Leave me, Iago.
Iago:	(*going*) My lord, I take my leave.
Othello:	Why did I marry? This honest creature doubtless
	Sees and knows more, much more, than he unfolds.
Iago:	(*returning*)
	My lord, I would I might entreat your honour
	To scan this thing no farther. Leave it to time.
	Although 'tis fit that Cassio have his place –
	For sure he fills it up with great ability –
	Yet, if you please to hold him off a while,
	You shall by that perceive him and his means.
	Note if your lady strain his entertainment
	With any strong or vehement importunity.
	Much will be seen in that. In the mean time,
	Let me be thought too busy in my fears –
	As worthy cause I have to fear I am –
	And hold her free, I do beseech your honour.
Othello:	Fear not my government.
Iago:	I once more take my leave.

MACBETH

*Cornered by his enemies, who are marching upon Dunsinane
Castle under the cover of branches plucked from Birnam Wood, and
left completely alone by the death of his conscience-stricken wife,
Macbeth reflects at this moment of crisis on the ultimate futility of
existence.*

Macbeth: Tomorrow, and tomorrow, and tomorrow
           Creeps in this petty pace from day to day
           To the last syllable of recorded time,
           And all our yesterdays have lighted fools
           The way to dusty death. Out, out, brief candle.
           Life's but a walking shadow, a poor player
           That struts and frets his hour upon the stage,
           And then is heard no more. It is a tale
           Told by an idiot, full of sound and fury,
           Signifying nothing.

SONNET 60

Time the Destroyer.

> Like as the waves make towards the pebbled
>   shore,
> So do our minutes hasten to their end,
> Each changing place with that which goes
>   before;
> In sequent toil all forwards do contend.
> Nativity, once in the main of light,
> Crawls to maturity, wherewith being crowned
> Crookèd eclipses 'gainst his glory fight,
> And time that gave doth now his gift confound.
> Time doth transfix the flourish set on youth,
> And delves the parallels in beauty's brow;
> Feeds on the rarities of nature's truth,
> And nothing stands but for his scythe to mow.
> >   And yet to times in hope my verse shall
> >   stand,
> >   Praising thy worth despite his cruel hand.

KING LEAR

ACT III: SCENE 2.

Defied by his daughters Goneril and Regan, King Lear, in a fury, turns his back on the warmth and shelter of Gloucester's castle and sets out obstinately into the gathering storm. He stands on the open heath and roars his challenge to the howling wind and the driving rain, the thunder and the lightning, for there is nothing which the elements can throw at him which the ingratitude of his children has not already achieved. Nature's tempest echoes the storm in his heart and the unnatural callousness of his daughters is mirrored in a world which seems on this violent night to be on the verge of an apocalyptic explosion.

Lear: Blow, winds, and crack your cheeks! Rage,
            blow,
           You cataracts and hurricanoes, spout
           Till you have drenched our steeples, drowned
             the cocks!
           You sulph'rous and thought-executing fires,
           Vaunt-couriers of oak-cleaving thunderbolts,
           Singe my white head; and thou all-shaking
             thunder,
           Strike flat the thick rotundity o'th' world,
           Crack nature's moulds, all germens spill at once
           That makes ingrateful man. . . .
           Rumble thy bellyful; spit, fire; spout, rain.
           Nor rain, wind, thunder, fire are my daughters.
           I tax not you, you elements, with unkindness.
           I never gave you kingdom, called you children.
           You owe me no subscription. Then let fall
           Your horrible pleasure. Here I stand your slave,
           A poor, infirm, weak and despised old man,
           But yet I call you servile ministers,
           That will with two pernicious daughters join
           Your high-engendered battles 'gainst a head
           So old and white as this. Oh, ho, 'tis foul!

PUBLIC
LIFE
AND
LEADERSHIP

'Visiting British troops in Saudi Arabia [during the Gulf War] and knowing that a friend of mine was commanding a regiment in the desert, I found that the words Shakespeare puts into the King's mouth became even more poignant to me. They say everything that ever needs to be said in such circumstances, no matter what age we live in.'

The Prince of Wales, Shakespeare Birthday Lecture, 1991.

HENRY V

ACT IV: PROLOGUE.

The vastly superior French host has shadowed Henry V's invading army on its weary trek though Normandy and has now intercepted it at Agincourt. Chorus sets the scene on the eve of the battle as Henry makes a tour of his bedraggled and demoralised troops – camped within earshot of the carousing, confident French – in an attempt to raise their spirits before a day which few of the English soldiers believe they will survive.

Chorus: Now entertain conjecture of a time
               When creeping murmur and the poring dark
               Fills the wide vessel of the universe.
               From camp to camp through the foul womb of
                   night
               The hum of either army stilly sounds,
               That the fixed sentinels almost receive
               The secret whispers of each other's watch.
               Fire answers fire, and through their paly flames
               Each battle sees the other's umbered face.
               Steed threatens steed, in high and boastful
                   neighs
               Piercing the night's dull ear, and from the tents
               The armourers, accomplishing the knights,
               With busy hammers closing rivets up,
               Give dreadful note of preparation.
               The country cocks do crow, the clocks do toll
               And the third hour of drowsy morning name.
               Proud of their numbers and secure in soul,
               The confident and overlusty French
               Do the low-rated English play at dice,
               And chide the cripple tardy-gaited night,
               Who like a foul and ugly witch doth limp
               So tediously away. The poor condemnèd
                   English,
               Like sacrifices, by their watchful fires

Sit patiently and inly ruminate
The morning's danger; and their gesture sad,
Investing lank lean cheeks and war-worn coats,
Presented them unto the gazing moon
So many horrid ghosts. O now, who will
     behold
The royal captain of this ruined band
Walking from watch to watch, from tent to
     tent,
Let him cry, 'Praise and glory on his head!'
For forth he goes and visits all his host,
Bids them good morrow with a modest smile
And calls them brothers, friends, and
     countrymen.
Upon his royal face there is no note
How dread an army hath enrounded him;
Nor doth he dedicate one jot of colour
Unto the weary and all-watchèd night,
But freshly looks and overbears attaint
With cheerful semblance and sweet majesty,
That every wretch, pining and pale before,
Beholding him, plucks comfort from his looks.
A largess universal, like the sun,
His liberal eye doth give to everyone,
Thawing cold fear, that mean and gentle all
Behold, as may unworthiness define,
A little touch of Harry in the night.
And so our scene must to the battle fly,
Where O for pity, we shall much disgrace,
With four or five most vile and ragged foils,
Right ill-disposed in brawl ridiculous,
The name of Agincourt. Yet sit and see,
Minding true things by what their mock'ries be.

HENRY V

ACT IV: SCENE 3.

Drawn up for battle, the armies now face each other. The French outnumber the English by five to one and in the face of such unequal odds, Henry's nobles wish that reinforcements could somehow be spirited from England. But the King rejoices in their puny numbers which offer greater glory to those who survive the day.

Warwick:	O that we now had here
	But one ten thousand of those men in England
	That do no work today.
King Harry:	What's he that wishes so?
	My cousin Warwick? No, my fair cousin.
	If we are marked to die, we are enough
	To do our country loss; and if to live,
	The fewer men, the greater share of honour.
	God's will, I pray thee wish not one man more.
	By Jove, I am not covetous for gold,
	Nor care I who doth feed upon my cost;
	It ernes me not if men my garments wear;
	Such outward things dwell not in my desires.
	But if it be a sin to covet honour
	I am the most offending soul alive.
	No, faith, my coz, wish not a man from England.
	God's peace, I would not lose so great an honour
	As one man more methinks would share from me
	For the best hope I have. O do not wish one more.
	Rather proclaim it presently through my host
	That he which hath no stomach to this fight,
	Let him depart. His passport shall be made
	And crowns for convoy put into his purse.

We would not die in that man's company
That fears his fellowship to die with us.
This day is called the Feast of Crispian.
He that outlives this day and comes safe home
Will stand a-tiptoe when this day is named
And rouse him at the name of Crispian.
He that shall see this day and live t'old age
Will yearly on the vigil feast his neighbours
And say, 'Tomorrow is Saint Crispian.'
Then will he strip his sleeve and show his scars
And say, 'These wounds I had on Crispin's
    day.'
Old men forget; yet all shall be forgot,
But he'll remember, with advantages,
What feats he did that day. Then shall our
    names,
Familiar in his mouth as household words –
Harry the King, Bedford and Exeter,
Warwick and Talbot, Salisbury and
    Gloucester –
Be in their flowing cups freshly remembered.
This story shall the good man teach his son,
And Crispin Crispian shall ne'er go by
From this day to the ending of the world
But we in it shall be rememberèd,
We few, we happy few, we band of brothers.
For he today that sheds his blood with me
Shall be my brother; be he ne'er so vile,
This day shall gentle his condition.
And gentlemen in England now abed
Shall think themselves accursed they were not
    here,
And hold their manhoods cheap whiles any
    speaks
That fought with us upon Saint Crispin's day.

HENRY IV

*Sleepless, careworn, broken in health, still troubled by rebellion in
the north and worried that his son and heir, the Prince of Wales,
persists in keeping bad company in the taverns of Eastcheap, Henry
IV envies the lot of ordinary people who can sleep so much more
soundly than a king.*

King Henry: How many thousands of my poorest subjects
             Are at this hour asleep? O sleep, O gentle
                sleep,
             Nature's soft nurse, how have I frighted thee,
             That thou no more wilt weigh my eyelids down
             And steep my senses in forgetfulness?
             Why rather, sleep, liest thou in smoky cribs,
             Upon uneasy pallets stretching thee,
             And hushed with buzzing night-flies to thy
                slumber,
             Than in the perfumed chambers of the great,
             Under the canopies of costly state,
             And lulled with sound of sweetest melody?
             O thou dull god, why li'st thou with the vile
             In loathsome beds, and leav'st the kingly couch
             A watch-case, or a common 'larum-bell?
             Wilt thou upon the high and giddy mast
             Seal up the ship-boy's eyes, and rock his brains
             In cradle of the rude imperious surge,
             And in the visitation of the winds,
             Who take the ruffian billows by the top,
             Curling their monstrous heads and hanging
                them
             With deafing clamour in the slippery clouds,
             That, with the hurly, death itself awakes?
             Canst thou, O partial sleep, give thy repose
             To the wet sea-boy in an hour so rude,
             And in the calmest and most stillest night,

With all appliances and means to boot,
Deny it to a king? Then happy low, lie down.
Uneasy lies the head that wears a crown.

HENRY IV

PART ONE – ACT II: SCENE 5.

Hal/Harry and his friend Poins have returned in triumph to their lair at the Boar's Head Tavern in Eastcheap, having put Falstaff and his craven colleagues to flight and relieved them of the booty they had just stolen. Characteristically Falstaff attempts to turn his shame into a deed of valour. When his tale is exposed as a tissue of lies, Falstaff swiftly suggests a game of charades in which he casts himself as the King upbraiding his errant son. Yet underneath the fun, true feelings emerge. Falstaff eloquently and passionately defends what he is while the Prince clearly suggests that the days of their friendship may be numbered.

Poins:	Welcome, Jack. Where hast thou been?
Sir John:	A plague of all cowards, I say, and a vengeance too, marry and amen! – Give me a cup of sack, boy. – Ere I lead this life long, I'll sew netherstocks, and mend them and foot them too. A plague of all cowards! – Give me a cup of sack, rogue. Is there no virtue extant?
	He drinketh
Prince Harry:	Didst thou never see Titan kiss a dish of butter – pitiful-hearted Titan – that melted at the sweet tale of the sun's? If thou didst, then behold that compound.
Sir John:	*(to Francis)* You rogue, here's lime in this sack too. There is nothing but roguery to be found in villainous man, yet a coward is worse than a cup of sack with lime in it. *(Exit Francis)* A villainous coward! Go thy ways, old Jack, die when thou wilt. If manhood, good manhood, be not forgot upon the face of the earth, then am I a shotten herring. There lives not three good men unhanged in England, and one of them is fat and grows old, God help the while. A bad world, I say. I would I were a weaver – I

could sing psalms, or anything. A plague of all cowards, I say still.

Prince Harry: How now, woolsack, what mutter you?

Sir John: A king's son! If I do not beat thee out of thy kingdom with a dagger of lath, and drive all thy subjects afore thee like a flock of wild geese, I'll never wear hair on my face more. You, Prince of Wales!

Prince Harry: Why, you whoreson round man, what's the matter?

Sir John: Are not you a coward? Answer me to that. And Poins there?

Poins: Zounds, ye fat paunch, an ye call me coward, by the Lord I'll stab thee.

Sir John: I call thee coward? I'll see thee damned ere I call thee coward, but I would give a thousand pound I could run as fast as thou canst. You are straight enough in the shoulders; you care not who sees your back. Call you that backing of your friends? A plague upon such backing! Give me them that will face me. Give me a cup of sack. I am a rogue if I drunk today.

Prince Harry: O villain, thy lips are scarce wiped since thou drunkest last.

Sir John: All is one for that.

> *He drinketh*

A plague of all cowards, still say I.

Prince Harry: What's the matter?

Sir John: What's the matter? There be four of us here have ta'en a thousand pound this day morning.

Prince Harry: Where is it, Jack, where is it?

Sir John: Where is it? Taken from us it is. A hundred upon poor four of us.

Prince Harry: What, a hundred, man?

Sir John: I am a rogue if I were not at half-sword with a dozen of them, two hours together. I have scaped by miracle. I am eight times thrust through the doublet, four through the hose, my

buckler cut through and through, my sword
hacked like a handsaw. *Ecce signum.*
He shows his sword
I never dealt better since I was a man. . . .

Prince Harry: What, fought you with them all?

Sir John: All? I know not what you call all, but if I fought
not with fifty of them, I am a bunch of radish.
If there were not two- or three-and-fifty upon
poor old Jack, then am I no two-legged
creature.

Prince Harry: Pray God you have not murdered some of
them.

Sir John: Nay, that's past praying for. I have peppered
two of them. Two I am sure I have paid – two
rogues in buckram suits. I tell thee what, Hal, if
I tell thee a lie, spit in my face, call me horse.
Thou knowest my old ward –
He stands as to fight
here I lay, and thus I bore my point. Four
rogues in buckram let drive at me.

Prince Harry: What, four? Thou saidst but two even now.

Sir John: Four, Hal, I told thee four.

Poins: Ay, ay, he said four.

Sir John: These four came all afront, and mainly thrust at
me. I made me no more ado, but took all their
seven points in my target, thus.
He wards himself with his buckler

Prince Harry: Seven? Why, there were but four even now.

Sir John: In buckram?

Poins: Ay, four in buckram suits.

Sir John: Seven, by these hilts, or I am a villain else.

Prince Harry: *(aside to Poins)* Prithee, let him alone. We shall
have more anon.

Sir John: Dost thou hear me, Hal?

Prince Harry: Ay, and mark thee too, Jack.

Sir John: Do so, for it is worth the listening to. These
nine in buckram that I told thee of –

Prince Harry: *(aside to Poins)* So, two more already.

Sir John:	Their points being broken –
Poins:	*(aside to the Prince)* Down fell their hose.
Sir John:	Began to give me ground. But I followed me close, came in foot and hand, and, with a thought, seven of the eleven I paid.
Prince Harry:	*(aside to Poins)* O monstrous! Eleven buckram men grown out of two!
Sir John:	But, as the devil would have it, three misbegotten knaves in Kendal green came at my back and let drive at me; for it was so dark, Hal, that thou couldst not see thy hand.
Prince Harry:	These lies are like their father that begets them – gross as a mountain, open, palpable. Why, thou clay-brained guts, thou knotty-pated fool, thou whoreson obscene greasy tallow-catch –
Sir John:	What, art thou mad? Art thou mad? Is not the truth the truth?
Prince Harry:	Why, how couldst thou know these men in Kendal green when it was so dark thou couldst not see thy hand? Come, tell us your reason. What sayst thou to this?
Poins:	Come, your reason, Jack, your reason.
Sir John:	What, upon compulsion? Zounds, an I were at the strappado, or all the racks in the world, I would not tell you on compulsion. Give you a reason on compulsion? If reasons were as plentiful as blackberries, I would give no man a reason upon compulsion, I.
Prince Harry:	I'll be no longer guilty of this sin. This sanguine coward, this bed-presser, this horse-back-breaker, this huge hill of flesh –
Sir John:	'Sblood, you starveling, you elf-skin, you dried neat's tongue, you bull's pizzle, you stock-fish – O, for breath to utter what is like thee! – you tailor's yard, you sheath, you bow-case, you vile standing tuck –
Prince Harry:	Well, breathe awhile, and then to't again, and

when thou hast tired thyself in base
comparisons, hear me speak but this.

Poins: Mark, Jack.

Prince Harry: We two saw you four set on four, and bound
them, and were masters of their wealth. – Mark
now how a plain tale shall put you down. –
Then did we two set on you four, and, with a
word, outfaced you from your prize, and have
it; yea, and can show it you here in the house.
And Falstaff, you carried your guts away as
nimbly, with as quick dexterity, and roared for
mercy, and still run and roared, as ever I heard
bull-calf. What a slave art thou, to hack thy
sword as thou hast done, and then say it was in
fight! What trick, what device, what starting-
hole canst thou now find out to hide thee from
this open and apparent shame?

Poins: Come, let's hear, Jack; what trick hast thou now?

Sir John: By the Lord, I knew ye as well as he that made
ye. Why, hear you, my masters. Was it for me
to kill the heir-apparent? Should I turn upon
the true prince? Why, thou knowest I am as
valiant as Hercules; but beware instinct. The
lion will not touch the true prince – instinct is a
great matter. I was now a coward on instinct. I
shall think the better of myself and thee during
my life – I for a valiant lion, and thou for a true
prince. But by the Lord, lads, I am glad you
have the money. – *(Calling)* Hostess, clap to the
doors. – Watch tonight, pray tomorrow.
Gallants, lads, boys, hearts of gold, all the titles
of good fellowship come to you! What, shall we
be merry, shall we have a play extempore? . . .

Prince Harry: Do thou stand for my father, and examine me
upon the particulars of my life.

Sir John: Shall I? Content. This chair shall be my state,
this dagger my sceptre, and this cushion my
crown.

He sits

Prince Harry: Thy state is taken for a joint-stool, thy golden sceptre for a leaden dagger, and thy precious rich crown for a pitiful bald crown.

Sir John: Well, an the fire of grace be not quite out of thee, now shalt thou be moved. Give me a cup of sack to make my eyes look red, that it may be thought I have wept; for I must speak in passion, and I will do it in King Cambyses' vein.

Prince Harry: (bowing) Well, here is my leg.

Sir John: And here is my speech. Stand aside, nobility.

. . .

Harry, I do not only marvel where thou spendest thy time, but also how thou art accompanied. For though the camomile, the more it is trodden on, the faster it grows, yet youth, the more it is wasted, the sooner it wears. That thou art my son I have partly thy mother's word, partly my own opinion, but chiefly a villainous trick of thine eye, and a foolish hanging of thy nether lip, that doth warrant me. If then thou be son to me, here lies the point. Why, being son to me, art thou so pointed at? Shall the blessed sun of heaven prove a micher, and eat blackberries? – A question not to be asked. Shall the son of England prove a thief, and take purses? – A question to be asked. There is a thing, Harry, which thou hast often heard of, and it is known to many in our land by the name of pitch. This pitch, as ancient writers do report, doth defile. So doth the company thou keepest. For Harry, now I do not speak to thee in drink, but in tears; not in pleasure, but in passion; not in words only, but in woes also. And yet there is a virtuous man whom I have often noted in thy company, but I know not his name.

Prince Harry: What manner of man, an it like your majesty?

Sir John: A goodly, portly man, i'faith, and a corpulent; of a cheerful look, a pleasing eye, and a most noble carriage; and, as I think, his age some fifty, or, by'r Lady, inclining to threescore. And now I remember me, his name is Falstaff. If that man should be lewdly given, he deceiveth me; for, Harry, I see virtue in his looks. If, then, the tree may be known by the fruit, as the fruit by the tree, then peremptorily I speak it – there is virtue in that Falstaff. Him keep with; the rest banish. And tell me now, thou naughty varlet, tell me, where hast thou been this month?

Prince Harry: Dost thou speak like a king? Do thou stand for me, and I'll play my father.

Sir John: *(standing)* Depose me! If thou dost it half so gravely, so majestically, both in word and matter, hang me up by the heels for a rabbit sucker, or a poulter's hare.

Prince Harry: *(sitting)* Well, here I am set.

Sir John: And here I stand. *(To the others)* Judge, my masters.

Prince Harry: Now, Harry, whence come you?

Sir John: My noble lord, from Eastcheap.

Prince Harry: The complaints I hear of thee are grievous.

Sir John: 'Sblood, my lord, they are false. *(To the others)* Nay, I'll tickle ye for a young prince, i'faith.

Prince Harry: Swearest thou, ungracious boy? Henceforth ne'er look on me. Thou art violently carried away from grace. There is a devil haunts thee in the likeness of an old fat man; a tun of man is thy companion. Why dost thou converse with that trunk of humours, that bolting-hutch of beastliness, that swollen parcel of dropsies, that huge bombard of sack, that stuffed cloak-bag of guts, that roasted Manningtree ox with the pudding in his belly, that reverend Vice,

that grey Iniquity, that father Ruffian, that
Vanity in Years? Wherein is he good, but to
taste sack and drink it? Wherein neat and
cleanly, but to carve a capon and eat it?
Wherein cunning, but in craft? Wherein crafty,
but in villainy? Wherein villainous, but in all
things? Wherein worthy, but in nothing?

Sir John: I would your grace would take me with you.
Whom means your grace?

Prince Harry: That villainous, abominable misleader of
youth, Falstaff; that old white-bearded Satan.

Sir John: My Lord, the man I know.

Prince Harry: I know thou dost.

Sir John: But to say I know more harm in him than in
myself were to say more than I know. That he
is old, the more the pity, his white hairs do
witness it. But that he is, saving your
reverence, a whoremaster, that I utterly deny.
If sack and sugar be a fault, God help the
wicked. If to be old and merry be a sin, then
many an old host that I know is damned. If to
be fat be to be hated, then Pharaoh's lean kine
are to be loved. No, my good lord, banish Peto,
banish Bardolph, banish Poins, but for sweet
Jack Falstaff, kind Jack Falstaff, true Jack
Falstaff, valiant Jack Falstaff, and therefore
more valiant being, as he is, old Jack Falstaff,
Banish not him thy Harry's company,
Banish not him thy Harry's company.
Banish plump Jack, and banish all the world.

Prince Harry: I do; I will.

HENRY V

ACT IV: SCENE 1.

*It is the early hours of the morning of Agincourt and the King
steals through the camp in disguise to talk openly to the common
soldiers and gauge their state of mind. Facing what they assume to
be certain death, the men reflect bitterly that they are likely to be
the hapless victims of the King's quarrel, inevitable sacrifices to his
ambitions. Somewhat chastened, Henry ponders on the futility of
pomp and ceremony and envies the reassuringly tranquil everyday
life of even his meanest subjects.*

King Harry: Upon the King.
        'Let us our lives, our souls, our debts, our care-
           full wives,
        Our children, and our sins, lay on the King.'
        We must bear all. O hard condition,
        Twin-born with greatness: subject to the breath
        Of every fool, whose sense no more can feel
        But his own wringing. What infinite heartsease
        Must kings neglect that private men enjoy?
        And what have kings that privates have not
           too,
        Save ceremony, save general ceremony?
        And what art thou, thou idol ceremony.
        What kind of god art thou, that suffer'st more
        Of mortal griefs than do thy worshippers?
        What are thy rents? What are thy comings-in?
        O ceremony, show me but thy worth.
        What is thy soul of adoration?
        Art thou aught else but place, degree, and
           form,
        Creating awe and fear in other men?
        Wherein thou art less happy, being feared,
        Than they in fearing.
        What drink'st thou oft, instead of homage
           sweet,

But poisoned flattery? O be sick, great
   greatness,
And bid thy ceremony give thee cure.
Think'st thou the fiery fever will go out
With titles blown from adulation?
Will it give place to flexure and low bending?
Canst thou, when thou command'st the
   beggar's knee,
Command the health of it? No, thou proud
   dream
That play'st so subtly with a king's repose;
I am a king that find thee, and I know
'Tis not the balm, the sceptre, and the ball,
The sword, the mace, the crown imperial,
The intertissued robe of gold and pearl,
The farcèd title running fore the king,
The throne he sits on, nor the tide of pomp
That beats upon the high shore of this
   world –
No, not all these, thrice-gorgeous ceremony,
Not all these, laid in bed majestical,
Can sleep so soundly as the wretched slave
Who with a body filled and vacant mind
Gets him to rest, crammed with distressful
   bread;
Never sees horrid night, the child of hell,
But like a lackey from the rise to set
Sweats in the eye of Phoebus, and all night
Sleeps in Elysium; next day, after dawn
Doth rise and help Hyperion to his horse,
And follows so the ever-running year
With profitable labour to his grave.
And but for ceremony such a wretch,
Winding up days with toil and nights with
   sleep,
Had the forehand and vantage of a king.
The slave, a member of the country's peace,
Enjoys it, but in gross brain little wots

What watch the King keeps to maintain the
   peace,
Whose hours the peasant best advantages.

THE
COUNTRY

'When I was younger . . . I felt a strong attachment to the soil of those places I loved best – Balmoral, in Scotland, and Sandringham, in Norfolk. As far as I was concerned, every tree, every hedgerow, every wet place, every mountain and river had a special, almost sacred, character of its own.'

The Prince of Wales, Highgrove, Portrait of an Estate, *1993.*

RICHARD II

John of Gaunt, young Richard II's much-respected uncle, lies on his death-bed. As he waits to give his final words of advice to the wayward nephew who has surrounded himself with corrupt and flattering courtiers, he reflects on the dire state of the once-great kingdom of England.

Gaunt: This royal throne of kings, this sceptred isle,
This earth of majesty, this seat of Mars,
This other Eden, demi-paradise,
This fortress built by nature for herself
Against infection and the hand of war,
This happy breed of men, this little world,
This precious stone set in the silver sea,
Which serves it in the office of a wall,
Or as a moat defensive to a house
Against the envy of less happier lands;
This blessèd plot, this earth, this realm, this
   England,
This nurse, this teeming womb of royal kings,
Feared by their breed and famous by their
  birth,
Renownèd for their deeds as far from home
For Christian service and true chivalry
As is the sepulchre, in stubborn Jewry,
Of the world's ransom, blessèd Mary's son;
This land of such dear souls, this dear dear
  land,
Dear for her reputation through the world,
Is now leased out – I die pronouncing it –
Like to a tenement or pelting farm.
England, bound in with the triumphant sea,
Whose rocky shore beats back the envious siege
Of wat'ry Neptune, is now bound in with
  shame,

With inky blots and rotten parchment bonds.
That England that was wont to conquer others
Hath made a shameful conquest of itself.
Ah, would the scandal vanish with my life,
How happy then were my ensuing death!

AS YOU LIKE IT

ACT II: SCENE 1 AND ACT III: SCENE 2.

*Despite the harshness of the climate and the rigours of the outdoor
life to which he has been banished by a younger brother's treachery,
Duke Senior finds greater fidelity in Nature than he ever did in the
double-dealing, supposedly civilised court. Elsewhere in the Forest
of Arden other refugees are not so contented. One-time court jester
Touchstone is making a similar comparison to his companion
Corin, a wise old shepherd. Touchstone, however, misses the
comforts of civilisation and he mocks Corin's simple, Nature-based
philosophy, crushing him with his verbal agility as they debate the
contrasts between urban and country life.*

Duke Senior: Now, my co-mates and brothers in exile,
                Hath not old custom made this life more sweet
                Than that of painted pomp? Are not these
                   woods
                More free from peril than the envious court?
                Here feel we not the penalty of Adam,
                The seasons' difference, as the icy fang
                And churlish chiding of the winter's wind,
                Which when it bites and blows upon my body
                Even till I shrink with cold, I smile, and say
                'This is no flattery. These are counsellors
                That feelingly persuade me what I am.'
                Sweet are the uses of adversity
                Which, like the toad, ugly and venomous,
                Wears yet a precious jewel in his head;
                And this our life, exempt from public haunt,
                Finds tongues in trees, books in the running
                   brooks,
                Sermons in stones, and good in everything.
Amiens: I would not change it. Happy is your grace
                That can translate the stubbornness of fortune
                Into so quiet and so sweet a style. . . .

Act III: Scene 2.

Enter Corin and Touchstone the clown

Corin: And how like you this shepherd's life, Master Touchstone?

Touchstone: Truly, shepherd, in respect of itself, it is a good life; but in respect that it is a shepherd's life, it is naught. In respect that it is solitary, I like it very well; but in respect that it is private, it is a very vile life. Now in respect it is in the fields, it pleaseth me well; but in respect it is not in the court, it is tedious. As it is a spare life, look you, it fits my humour well; but as there is no more plenty in it, it goes much against my stomach. Hast any philosophy in thee, shepherd?

Corin: No more but that I know the more one sickens, the worse at ease he is, and that he that wants money, means, and content is without three good friends; that the property of rain is to wet, and fire to burn; that good pasture makes fat sheep; and that a great cause of the night is lack of the sun; that he that hath learned no wit by nature nor art may complain of good breeding or comes of a very dull kindred.

Touchstone: Such a one is a natural philosopher. Wast ever in court, shepherd?

Corin: No, truly.

Touchstone: Then thou art damned.

Corin: Nay, I hope.

Touchstone: Truly thou art damned, like an ill-roasted egg, all on one side.

Corin: For not being at court? Your reason?

Touchstone: Why, if thou never wast at court thou never sawest good manners. If thou never sawest good manners, then thy manners must be wicked, and wickedness is sin, and sin is damnation. Thou art in a parlous state, shepherd.

Corin:	Not a whit, Touchstone. Those that are good manners at the court are as ridiculous in the country as the behaviour in the country is most mockable at the court. You told me you salute not at the court but you kiss your hands. That courtesy would be uncleanly if courtiers were shepherds.
Touchstone:	Instance, briefly; come, instance.
Corin:	Why, we are still handling our ewes, and their fells, you know, are greasy.
Touchstone:	Why, do not your courtier's hands sweat? And is not the grease of a mutton as wholesome as the sweat of a man? Shallow, shallow. A better instance, I say. Come.
Corin:	Besides, our hands are hard.
Touchstone:	Your lips will feel them the sooner. Shallow again. A more sounder instance. Come.
Corin:	And they are often tarred over with the surgery of our sheep; and would you have us kiss tar? The courtier's hands are perfumed with civet.
Touchstone:	Most shallow, man. Thou worms' meat in respect of a good piece of flesh indeed, learn of the wise, and perpend: civet is of a baser birth than tar, the very uncleanly flux of a cat. Mend the instance, shepherd.
Corin:	You have too courtly a wit for me. I'll rest.

RICHARD II

*Shakespeare reveals in several places his knowledge of gardening.
In this scene in Gloucestershire news has yet to reach the Queen
that her husband, Richard II, has been forced to abdicate and
surrender the crown to Bolingbroke. In a fever of anxiety she
wanders about the garden, and when the gardeners appear she
eavesdrops on their conversation. They are much better informed
than she is: they have heard of Richard's downfall and of the
execution of his corrupt associates. The garden becomes a useful
metaphor for the kingdom and a gardener's duties for the
responsibilities of kingship.*

Gardener:	*(to First Man)* Go, bind thou up young dangling apricots
	Which, like unruly children, make their sire
	Stoop with oppression of their prodigal weight.
	Give some supportance to the bending twigs.
	(To Second Man) Go thou, and, like an executioner,
	Cut off the heads of too fast-growing sprays
	That look too lofty in our commonwealth.
	All must be even in our government.
	You thus employed, I will go root away
	The noisome weeds which without profit suck
	The soil's fertility from wholesome flowers.
First Man:	Why should we, in the compass of a pale,
	Keep law and form and due proportion,
	Showing as in a model our firm estate,
	When our sea-wallèd garden, the whole land,
	Is full of weeds, her fairest flowers choked up,
	Her fruit trees all unpruned, her hedges ruined,
	Her knots disordered, and her wholesome herbs

	Swarming with caterpillars?
Gardener:	Hold thy peace.

He that hath suffered this disordered spring
Hath now himself met with the fall of leaf.
The weeds which his broad spreading leaves
   did shelter,
That seemed in eating him to hold him up,
Are plucked up, root and all, by Bolingbroke –
I mean the Earl of Wiltshire, Bushy, Green.

Second Man: What, are they dead?

Gardener: They are; and Bolingbroke
Hath seized the wasteful King. O, what pity is
   it
That he had not so trimmed and dressed his
   land
As we this garden! We at time of year
Do wound the bark, the skin of our fruit trees,
Lest, being over-proud in sap and blood,
With too much riches it confound itself.
Had he done so to great and growing men,
They might have lived to bear, and he to taste,
Their fruits of duty. Superfluous branches
We lop away, that bearing boughs may live.
Had he done so, himself had borne the crown,
Which waste of idle hours hath quite thrown
   down.

MUSIC
AND
ACTING

'In every age of our history, poets and painters, musicians and dramatists have transformed crude fact into human meaning, adding new regions to the kingdom of the imagination.'

The Prince of Wales, Shakespeare Birthday Lecture, 1991.

TWELFTH NIGHT

Act I: Scene 1.

Orsino, the Duke of Illyria, is prey to an unrequited passion for his beautiful neighbour, the Countess Olivia. Her brother has died recently and so painfully does she feel his loss that she has decided to withdraw from the world and observe seven years of mourning. She refuses to see Orsino or any of his representatives and will not accept any tokens of his love. Orsino, who has a weakness for self-dramatisation, is thoroughly indulging himself – his capricious nature ordering and then abandoning a programme of continuous music, the therapy which he hopes will cure him of his infatuation. If he grows tired of music through over-exposure to it then surely, he deduces, he will also grow tired of love.

Orsino: If music be the food of love, play on,
              Give me excess of it that, surfeiting,
              The appetite may sicken and so die.
              That strain again, it had a dying fall.
              O, it came o'er my ear like the sweet sound
              That breathes upon a bank of violets,
              Stealing and giving odour. Enough, no more,
              'Tis not sweet now as it was before.
                 Music ceases
              O spirit of love, how quick and fresh art thou
              That, notwithstanding thy capacity
              Receiveth as the sea, naught enters there,
              Of what validity and pitch so e'er,
              But falls into abatement and low price
              Even in a minute! So full of shapes is fancy
              That it alone is high fantastical.

A MIDSUMMER NIGHT'S DREAM

Act I: Scene 2 and Act III: Scene 1.

Peter Quince, a carpenter, gathers a company of fellow Athenian tradesmen at his house. Amateur actors of varying degrees of enthusiasm and ability, they are to present a performance of a play based on the tragic love story of Pyramus and Thisbe as part of the celebrations which will follow the marriage of Duke Theseus to Hippolyta, Queen of the Amazons. Nick Bottom, the troupe's leading man, is not satisfied with the role of Pyramus alone and suggests himself for other parts as well. Peter Quince, the producer stands firm and they agree to rehearse in the Palace Wood the next evening.

Quince:	Is all our company here?
Bottom:	You were best to call them generally, man by man, according to the scrip.
Quince:	Here is the scroll of every man's name which is thought fit through all Athens to play in our interlude before the Duke and the Duchess on his wedding day at night.
Bottom:	First, good Peter Quince, say what the play treats on; then read the names of the actors; and so grow to a point.
Quince:	Marry, our play is *The Most Lamentable Comedy and Most Cruel Death of Pyramus and Thisbe.*
Bottom:	A very good piece of work, I assure you, and a merry. Now, good Peter Quince, call forth your actors by the scroll. Masters, spread yourselves.
Quince:	Answer as I call you. Nick Bottom, the weaver?
Bottom:	Ready. Name what part I am for, and proceed.
Quince:	You, Nick Bottom, are set down for Pyramus.
Bottom:	What is Pyramus? A lover or a tyrant?
Quince:	A lover, that kills himself most gallant for love.
Bottom:	That will ask some tears in the true performing of it. If I do it, let the audience look to their eyes. I will move stones. I will condole, in some

measure. To the rest. – Yet my chief humour is
for a tyrant. I could play 'erc'les rarely, or a part
to tear a cat in, to make all split.

> The raging rocks
> And shivering shocks
> Shall break the locks
> Of prison gates,
> And Phibbus' car
> Shall shine from far
> And make and mar
> The foolish Fates.

This was lofty. Now name the rest of the
players. – This is 'erc'les' vein, a tyrant's vein.
A lover is more condoling.

Quince:	Francis Flute, the bellows-mender?
Flute:	Here, Peter Quince.
Quince:	Flute, you must take Thisbe on you.
Flute:	What is Thisbe? A wand'ring knight?
Quince:	It is the lady that Pyramus must love.
Flute:	Nay, faith, let not me play a woman. I have a beard coming.
Quince:	That's all one. You shall play it in a mask, and you may speak as small as you will.
Bottom:	An I may hide my face, let me play Thisbe too. I'll speak in a monstrous little voice: 'Thisne, Thisne!' – 'Ah, Pyramus, my lover dear, thy Thisbe dear and lady dear.'
Quince:	No, no, you must play Pyramus; and Flute, you Thisbe.
Bottom:	Well, proceed.
Quince:	Robin Starveling, the tailor?
Starveling:	Here, Peter Quince.
Quince:	Robin Starveling, you must play Thisbe's mother. Tom Snout, the tinker?
Snout:	Here, Peter Quince.
Quince:	You, Pyramus' father; myself, Thisbe's father. Snug the joiner, you the lion's part; and I hope here is a play fitted.

Snug:	Have you the lion's part written? Pray you, if it be, give it me; for I am slow of study.
Quince:	You may do it extempore, for it is nothing but roaring.
Bottom:	Let me play the lion too. I will roar that I will do any man's heart good to hear me. I will roar that I will make the Duke say 'Let him roar again; let him roar again.'
Quince:	An you should do it too terribly you would fright the Duchess and the ladies that they would shriek, and that were enough to hang us all.
All the rest:	That would hang us, every mother's son.
Bottom:	I grant you, friends, if you should fright the ladies out of their wits they would have no more discretion but to hang us, but I will aggravate my voice so that I will roar you as gently as any sucking dove. I will roar you an 'twere any nightingale.
Quince:	You can play no part but Pyramus; for Pyramus is a sweet-faced man; a proper man as one shall see in a summer's day; a most lovely, gentlemanlike man. Therefore you must needs play Pyramus.
Bottom:	Well, I will undertake it. What beard were I best to play it in?
Quince:	Why, what you will.
Bottom:	I will discharge it in either your straw-colour beard, your orange-tawny beard, your purple-in-grain beard, or your French-crown-colour beard, your perfect yellow.
Quince:	Some of your French crowns have no hair at all, and then you will play bare faced. But masters, here are your parts, and I am to entreat you, request you, and desire you to con them by tomorrow night, and meet me in the palace wood a mile without the town by moonlight. There will we rehearse; for if we meet in the

	city we shall be dogged with company, and our devices known. In the meantime I will draw a bill of properties such as our play wants. I pray you fail me not.
Bottom:	We will meet, and there we may rehearse most obscenely and courageously. Take pains; be perfect. Adieu.
Quince:	At the Duke's oak we meet.
Bottom:	Enough. Hold, or cut bowstrings.

Act III: Scene 1

By the time the 'rude mechanicals' meet in the wood for their first rehearsal of Pyramus and Thisbe, *Bottom, the leading man, has scrutinised the text and has a number of alterations and additions to suggest. The vigour with which these are debated attracts the attention of Robin Goodfellow, or Puck, who seizes the opportunity, as the rehearsal begins, to make mischief by magically transforming Bottom's head into that of an ass.*

	Enter the clowns: Quince, Snug, Bottom, Flute, Snout, and Starveling.
Bottom:	Are we all met?
Quince:	Pat, pat; and here's a marvellous convenient place for our rehearsal. This green plot shall be our stage, this hawthorn brake our tiring-house, and we will do it in action as we will do it before the Duke.
Bottom:	Peter Quince?
Quince:	What sayst thou, bully Bottom?
Bottom:	There are things in this comedy of Pyramus and Thisbe that will never please. First, Pyramus must draw a sword and kill himself, which the ladies cannot abide. How answer you that?
Snout:	By'r la'kin, a parlous fear.
Starveling:	I believe we must leave the killing out, when all is done.
Bottom:	Not a whit. I have a device to make all well.

130

Write me a prologue, and let the prologue seem
to say we will do no harm with our swords,
and that Pyramus is not killed indeed; and for
the more better assurance, tell them that I,
Pyramus, am not Pyramus, but Bottom the
weaver. This will put them out of fear.

Quince: Well, we will have such a prologue; and it shall
be written in eight and six.

Bottom: No, make it two more: let it be written in eight
and eight.

Snout: Will not the ladies be afeard of the lion?

Starveling: I fear it, I promise you.

Bottom: Masters, you ought to consider with yourself,
to bring in – God shield us – a lion among
ladies is a most dreadful thing; for there is not a
more fearful wild fowl than your lion living,
and we ought to look to't.

Snout: Therefore another prologue must tell he is not a
lion.

Bottom: Nay, you must name his name, and half his
face must be seen through the lion's neck, and
he himself must speak through, saying thus or
to the same defect: 'ladies', or 'fair ladies, I
would wish you' or 'I would request you' or 'I
would entreat you not to fear, not to tremble.
My life for yours. If you think I come hither as
a lion, it were pity of my life. No, I am no such
thing. I am a man, as other men are' – and
there, indeed, let him name his name, and tell
them plainly he is Snug the joiner.

Quince: Well, it shall be so; but there is two hard things:
that is, to bring the moonlight into a chamber –
for you know Pyramus and Thisbe meet by
moonlight.

Snout: Doth the moon shine that night we play our
play?

Bottom: A calendar, a calendar – look in the almanac,
find out moonshine, find out moonshine.

131

Enter Robin Goodfellow the puck, invisible

Quince: *(with a book)* Yes, it doth shine that night.

Bottom: Why, then may you leave a casement of the great chamber window where we play open, and the moon may shine in at the casement.

Quince: Ay, or else one must come in with a bush of thorns and a lantern and say he comes to disfigure, or to present, the person of Moonshine. Then there is another thing: we must have a wall in the great chamber; for Pyramus and Thisbe, says the story, did talk through the chink of a wall.

Snout: You can never bring in a wall. What say you, Bottom?

Bottom: Some man or other must present Wall; and let him have some plaster, or some loam, or some rough-cast about him, to signify 'wall'; and let him hold his fingers thus, and through that cranny shall Pyramus and Thisbe whisper.

Quince: If that may be, then all is well. Come, sit down every mother's son, and rehearse your parts. Pyramus, you begin. When you have spoken your speech, enter into that brake; and so everyone according to his cue.

Robin: *(aside)* What hempen homespuns have we swagg'ring here
So near the cradle of the Fairy Queen?
What, a play toward? I'll be an auditor –
An actor, too, perhaps, if I see cause.

Quince: Speak, Pyramus. Thisbe, stand forth.

Bottom: *(as Pyramus)* Thisbe, the flowers of odious savours sweet.

Quince: Odours, odours.

Bottom: *(as Pyramus)*   Odours savours sweet.
So hath thy breath, my dearest Thisbe dear.
But hark, a voice. Stay thou but here a while,
And by and by I will to thee appear.

Exit

Robin:	*(aside)* A stranger Pyramus than e'er played here.

Exit

Flute:	Must I speak now?
Quince:	Ay, marry must you. For you must understand he goes but to see a noise that he heard, and is to come again.
Flute:	*(as Thisbe)* Most radiant Pyramus, most lily-white of hue,
	Of colour like the red rose on triumphant brier;
	Most bristly juvenile, and eke most lovely Jew,
	As true as truest horse that yet would never tire:
	I'll meet thee, Pyramus, at Ninny's tomb.
Quince:	Ninus' tomb, man! – Why, you must not speak that yet. That you answer to Pyramus. You speak all your part at once, cues and all. – Pyramus, enter: your cue is past; it is 'never tire'.
Flute:	O.
	(as Thisbe) As true as truest horse that yet would never tire.

Enter Robin leading Bottom with the ass-head

Bottom:	*(as Pyramus)* If I were fair, Thisbe, I were only thine.
Quince:	O monstrous! O strange! We are haunted. Pray, masters; fly, masters: help!

EPILOGUE

THE TEMPEST

Act IV: Scene 1.

*To celebrate the betrothal of his daughter Miranda to the ship-
wrecked Ferdinand, Prince of Naples, Prospero conjures up a
Masque performed by some of the Spirits whom his magic can
command. At the end the enchanting spectacle vanishes as quickly
and mysteriously as it took shape – an apt metaphor for life and
art. This speech is sometimes taken to be Shakespeare's own
farewell to the stage.*

Prospero: Our revels now are ended. These our actors,
As I foretold you, were all spirits, and
Are melted into air, into thin air;
And like the baseless fabric of this vision,
The cloud-capped towers, the gorgeous
   palaces,
The solemn temples, the great globe itself,
Yea, all which it inherit, shall dissolve;
And, like this insubstantial pageant faded,
Leave not a rack behind. We are such stuff
As dreams are made on, and our little life
Is rounded with a sleep.